Rector's Ramblings

By: Sarah Manouch

Table of Contents

3

Dedications

This book is dedicated to the memory of my parents, Charles (Charlie) and Kathleen (Kit) Manouch, and to my sister, Kathryn.

Mum and Dad taught me to respect others, to treat others as I would wish to be treated, and to be content. To value what I have, not to envy, and to appreciate the simple things of life. They also taught me, through their example, of the value of hard work, determination, and commitment to what I believe in.

It is only because of the support of my sister that I have been able to fulfil my calling to serve God. Without her help I would not be where I am, or who I am, today.

Acknowledgments

This selection of Rambles would not have seen the light of day, in book form, were it not for the positive feedback, and some constructive criticism, from the people who first received them – the people of the parish of East Dean, Singleton and West Dean (The Valley Parish), and beyond.

I also want to thank, and acknowledge, the people who got me where I am today in my ministry; my fellow students, and the staff, at SEITE (South East Institute of Theological Education), now St Augustine's College of Theology. From day one of my training, way back in September 2012, the students and staff were friendly, supportive, helpful, and very, very, understanding as we all faced the challenges and difficulties of part time study. Special thanks go to Sara-Jane Stevens, my roommate for weekend residentials, who made the journeys to various locations across the South-East of England both fun and informative, and made sure I got to breakfast on time. To Helen Reeves, for all her encouragement when things became overwhelming, for continuing to be my friend and pilgrimage companion, and for the fantastic lunches where we put the world to right. And to Simon Stocks, Biblical Studies tutor, staff tutor, and mentor. Without Simon's inspiration I would never have completed my studies, and without his invaluable input during my curacy years I would probably never have had the confidence and courage to become a parish priest. My years at SEITE also taught me the value of variety in worship, the importance of always being open to a different point of view, and, after 20 plus written assignments, how to string a sentence together that makes sense.

Special thanks also go to Prior Andrew Johnson, OSB. Prior Andrew was my Spiritual Director as I underwent the time of discernment prior to ordination training. His response to my frequent self-doubting question of 'Why me?' was a very definite 'Why not you?' which encouraged me to continue with my calling and to believe in myself.

And finally, I would like to thank Nigel and Jo Carter. During my years as a Curate, Nigel and Jo provided a place of refuge and refreshment (and I don't just mean Jo's delicious lunches) when it all seemed too much, and their belief in me, and my ministry, provided me with the self confidence and assurance I needed to serve my curacy parish, and to become the priest I am today.

About the Author

Sarah Manouch was born in Chichester and lived there until her move to Singleton in 2020. She attended St James' Church of England Primary School, before moving up to Chichester High School for Girls. After leaving school, she began work for a local Pension and Administration company, initially with the intention of obtaining a few years office and work experience. However, job changes, promotions, and restructuring, all of which offered new challenges and opportunities, resulted in her staying with the company for 25 years. Redundancy in 2009 proved to be a turning point, as after years of resisting and trying to ignore a call to ordained ministry, she accepted God's call and began the discernment process that saw her accepted for training at SEITE (South East Institute of Theological Education).

She began her training in 2012 and after graduation was made Deacon in the Church of England on 27th June 2015 at Chichester Cathedral. She served her Curacy in the parishes of West Wittering with Birdham and Itchenor, and after twelve months was ordained Priest by Bishop Martin Warner. Her curacy ended in 2018, but she continued in the parish as an Associate Priest until 2020. It was during the

11

first Covid 19 Lockdown that the position of House for Duty Incumbent for the Parish of East Dean, Singleton, and West Dean became available and after a nerve-wracking Zoom interview, Sarah was appointed to the post.

As well as serving as a Parish Priest, Sarah is also the Deputy Manager of St Olav's Christian Bookshop in Chichester. Sarah sees the bookshop as another part of her ministry, as it provides the opportunity to talk with customers and visitors about their faith, and also to offer help and support. Sarah also serves as a Day Chaplain in Chichester Cathedral, where as well as hourly prayers from the Pulpit, she also prays with visitors, talks to everyone, and even offers tourist information and advice on what to see and where to go in her favourite city.

Introduction

This collection of 'Rector's Ramblings' began life during the unforgettable times between Covid lockdowns in 2020. Having just been licenced as a House for Duty Priest in the Parish of East Dean, Singleton, and West Dean (the Valley parish) and unable to meet my parishioners in person, I began sending out a newsletter. These soon turned into me rambling on about life in the Rectory, events in the news, local and national, trivial and momentous, and the natural world surrounding us.

These musings on life in a rural Rectory cover events including the death of Queen Elizabeth II, the coronation of her son, natural disasters, and the mundane day-to-day life of a Priest, part-time Assistant Manager of a Christian Bookshop, and occasional Cathedral Day Chaplain.

Some will make you think, some will make you smile, and one or two may make you cry, but I hope all will help bring you closer to God.

20th December 2020

My First Christmas in the Valley Parish

I don't know about you, but I love Christmas movies. It's a Wonderful Life, Miracle of 34th Street, and Love Actually are all brilliant, but my all-time favourite Christmas movie is A Muppet Christmas Carol! It's the first movie I watch to put me in the Christmas spirit every year, and I know most of the songs and joyously sing along.

It's full of all the usual Muppet favourite characters and a wonderful Scrooge played by Michael Caine. I will never know how he kept a straight face when shouting at a Kermit Bob Cratchit.

There are two songs in the film I particularly love. The first is sung by the Ghost of Christmas Present as he takes Scrooge out onto the streets of London on Christmas Morning, and the second is sung by Scrooge as he begins what can only be described as his rehabilitation into the human race.

On Christmas morning, the meaning of Christmas is summed up beautifully in the chorus of 'Where love is found, it feels like Christmas.'

14

It is the season of the heart, A special time of caring

The ways of love made clear

It is the season of the spirit

The message, if we hear it, is make it last all year

Then, as Scrooge looks to a more hopeful, generous, and loving future, he sings gratitude and prayer in his 'Thankful Heart.'

With a thankful heart, With an endless joy

With a growing family. Every girl and boy

Will be nephew and niece to me

Will bring love, hope, and peace to me

Yes, and every night will end, and every day will start.

With a grateful prayer and a thankful heart

As we look to Christmas Day and beyond, I pray that we all hear and feel the message of the season of the heart and that every night and every day will end with a grateful prayer and a thankful heart.

26th February 2021

So now we have a roadmap, a direction, out of lockdowns, out of social distancing, out of the worst effects of the Pandemic, but even this comes with caveats, 'no earlier than...'. We still need to be on our guard against another wave of infections; we still need to take care of ourselves and each other, but we are heading in the right direction.

But in thinking about the roadmap, about the fact that we are now able to start planning, to start looking forward, I reflected on the fact that although God gives us signs and signposts, although He offers us pointers and even helpful people along the way to give us directions, He leaves the choice as to whether we follow those signs and directions up to us. In the Lent Group this week, we heard from the Archbishop of Canterbury about the fact that God leaves us space to go our own way, to decide not to listen to Him, not to follow him.

During the time of discernment, before accepting God's call to ordination, I commented to a friend that I really wish God had email or access to a letter box so that He could tell me clearly what He wanted me to do. I wanted something tangible, something definite so that I could say, 'OK, now I understand.' But, of course, that didn't happen. I was guided by friends, by clergy, by that 'still small voice,' and then, as I prepared to begin my Curacy in West Wittering, I was offered a basket of shells, each with a bible passage on it, to choose one at random.....or maybe not. The one I chose and put straight in my pocket was Proverbs 3: 3 – 5

'Trust in the Lord with your heart, and lean not on your own understanding,
in all your ways acknowledge Him, and He will make your paths straight.'

It is my favourite bible passage and a wonderful affirmation for a newly ordained Curate to receive, but as with the roadmap, it comes with caveats. If we follow God, trust in God, He will make our paths straight, but He doesn't promise that it will be flat, or pothole-free, or an easy path to follow. The path will still have side roads that will tempt us away from God and still have times of doubt, fear, and great joy. Our job, as Christians, is to discern the path God is calling us to walk on and to be prepared to walk it confidently and invite others to walk it with us.

So, as we look to the future, as we as a family of faith look to what God is calling us all to do and be in The Valley parish, I would like to offer you two prayers.

The first, The Serenity Prayer, has, I know, been of great comfort and support to many over the past year,

God grant me the serenity to accept the things I cannot change;
Courage to change the things I can, and wisdom to know the difference.

The second is a prayer from the Church Times way back in 1982, which was found in a Parish Magazine when we finished clearing the house in Chichester.

Lord, help me not to dread what might happen,
Nor to worry about what could happen,
But to accept what does happen
Because you care for me.
Amen

One of my favourite scenes in any movie is in Notting Hill when the passing of a year is marked by Hugh Grant walking through the market as the weather changes. We go through all the seasons, starting in summer (with a pregnant lady at one end of the street) and ending up in summer again (with the same lady now holding a newborn baby).

The weather can and usually does, have a huge impact on our lives. The changing of the seasons often dictates what we do and when. But how many of us would move halfway around the world twice because of the weather? Well, that's exactly what a former work colleague of mine did many years ago.

Announcing he and his family were off to Australia, he cited the weather as one of the reasons, along with a great new job, a wonderful house, and beautiful beaches. Imagine our surprise when less than 5 years later they were back, not just for a visit but to stay. Yes, the job had been all he hoped, the house had been amazing, and the beaches a second home to them, but they had missed the seasons. They missed early morning frosts, they missed getting wet in unexpected showers on country walks, and they missed the joy and uncertainty of a British summer's day. Would it stay dry? Was the temperature going to break records? Morning to evening sun was great for a while, but it wasn't for them. Now, to be fair, I also know people who have moved to Oz and absolutely love it because of the weather!

But our weather is changing, and as many countries, especially in the West, look beyond Covid, Climate Change is once again high on the agenda. April was, according to the

Met Office, the frostiest April on record and also the driest, with very few April showers. Frost in May was practically unheard of only a few years ago, and certainly not snow, but even in The Valley, I was welcomed home from work on Wednesday by (a brief) hail storm!

The big question for many is why is our weather changing? Is it global warming, or is it just because that's what it does? After all, much of our countryside has been shaped by the Ice Ages, and animal species have been extinct for millennia because of the natural changes in the weather. But this is different. Australia is getting hotter every year; our seasons are frequently out of kilter, the seas are rising, and the ice cap is melting. Much of it is down to us and our recent ancestors of the industrial age.

The first lockdown saw nature reclaiming some of its own. Even sheep and goats reclaimed, albeit temporarily, old grazing land that was now full of housing. As we look to the end of restrictions and a return to normality, this is also a time to relook at our role as stewards of God's creation. Whether we invest in solar panels or an electric car, whether we forgo plastic or buy organic or sustainably sourced foods, we all have our part to play in fulfilling the 5th of the 5 Marks of Mission for the Church - 'To strive to safeguard the integrity of creation and sustain and renew the life of the earth.' This isn't a call to save the planet; the planet will survive whatever happens. This is a call to save every living thing that exists on the planet – this is God's call to us, as his chosen people, to lead the way and to leave a richer, more diverse creation for future generations.

21st May 2021

Do you ever find yourself with a funny kind of obsession that you don't really understand but that takes over a large part of your day, your week, or maybe longer?

A couple of years ago, in the wilds of West Yorkshire, I got obsessed with steps (and no, I don't mean the 90's pop group). I was on a silent, guided retreat at the Community of the Resurrection in Mirfield, and on the first day, my retreat guide, Father Oswin, told me to just 'go for a wander' around the grounds, get my bearings, and try and put out of my mind all the jobs I had left undone at home, all the emails I had left answered, and just see what I found.

Well, one of the first things I found was a set of steps leading to an annoyingly locked door under the main church, and that got me started on my quest for steps. I climbed the steps down to the Cemetery and the steps out of the quarry. I found steps in the sunshine and steps in the rain.

Every morning, I would go hunting new steps, to climb them, to photograph them, and then to proudly tell Father Oswin, 'I found more of your steps today'! He would then confidently declare, 'But not all of them!'. My claim on the last day that I had found ALL their steps got a slightly wry smile and shake of the head, so I suspect there are secret steps known only to him, but I will go back, and I WILL find them!

But what did it all mean? Well, I was on retreat, I was withdrawn from the world, I was reflecting on my life, my faith, and my calling, and the steps seemed to mirror my own reflections. On days of questioning and doubt, I found steps that went down in shadow or rain. On other days, a lightened mood found steps that went up were wide, open sunlight!

Life is like those steps, sometimes hard to climb, sometimes easy, sometimes direct, sometimes winding, sometimes lit by sunlight, sometimes wet with rain, or maybe tears, but all steps, as all life, are part of God's creation, God's world, and with His help, we can climb them all, whether up or down, easy or steep.

As we head, albeit slowly, out of Covid restrictions, it is good to remember the steps, the hurdles we have all overcome, the loved ones we have lost, and to remember the most important steps I climbed that week – three granite blocks at the foot of the cross in the garden they call Calvary.

25th June 2021
The longest day? More like the coldest!

The summer solstice on Monday marked the longest day of the year with, allegedly, almost 17 hours of sunshine! Well, it wasn't that sunny, and it wasn't that warm! But then looking for a silver lining, it meant I had an excuse to dig out my trusty hot water bottle again! It may be considered by some to be old fashioned but there is something comforting and reassuring about snuggling up with a fluffy hot water bottle. Be it on the sofa to watch an old movie, or in bed to read a good book, the act of hugging the bottle, or feeling the warmth rising from the bottle at your feet, gives a sense that all is right with the world. It is always with great reluctance that I put it away at the end of the winter.

But there is something else I reach for as I settle down for the night, and that is my holding cross. Made of olive wood from the Holy Land it is shaped to fit neatly, and comfortably, into the palm of the hand. Some carry a cross with them everywhere, in their pocket or in their bag, ready for when it is needed. I have known people take their crosses into the operating theatre with them, the nurses and surgeons well aware of the benefits to the patient, and often to their families, of having that simple piece of wood held tightly as

24

the anaesthetic takes effect, and then resting gently in the palm during the operation. I also know that many nurses will make sure it is there, still in the hand, once surgery is over.

I carry a cross in my bag, but the cross beside my bed is special. It is special because no matter how much I toss and turn in the night, in the morning it is never far from my side. It is special because it reminds me that the last words I say at night, out loud or to myself, should be directed to God. But it is also special because it is usually in the long hours of the night that most of us are beset by our fears and our doubts, and holding on to a cross, be it olive wood, a rosary, or a remembered image from a favourite church or place, helps calm the mind and soothe the soul. Whatever you find comforting in these continuing times of uncertainty—a hot water bottle, a holding cross, a walk in the woods, or an hour in the garden—I pray that we will all remember that our greatest comforter, our greatest source of hope, peace and calm, is our God in heaven, who is there in the daytime, in the nighttime, in the good times and in the bad, holding us in His loving embrace.

2nd July 2021
Second choice is sometimes the best choice...

It came as no real surprise last week when our travel company contacted us to say, sorry, your holiday has had to be cancelled. If we're honest, it was actually a little bit of a relief, after what can only be described as a topsy turvy year, with pandemics, and house moves, and stop-start work life, did we really want the hassle of airports, and luggage limits, of the uncertainty of will we have to quarantine on the outward, and possibly inward, journeys! So yes, we're disappointed that the holiday planned for last year still can't happen, but the money is sitting safely in an ABTA-protected bank account, waiting for us to decide if, and where, we will go next year, or maybe the year after, and we are still getting a break away, just to our second choice, a few days in Somerset.

But maybe a pressure-free holiday in this country is actually what we need. Maybe our second choice is actually the right choice. I am currently reading a book called *Singing in Babylon* which is looking at the Book of Daniel, and the fact that Daniel and his friends actually made the best of their life in exile, did the best they could for the people that they had to serve, rather than bemoan the loss of their first-choice life, that of the rich and privileged in their homeland. For many of us, we have to accept at some point that our lives have maybe not turned out the way we had hoped, the way we had planned. Maybe we planned, hoped, for an illustrious career as a professional footballer or tennis player, but it didn't happen. Maybe our plans were for a career in the military, or as a chef, or to have a family, but it didn't happen.

There is a wonderful quote from Woody Allen which says 'If you want to make God laugh, tell him your plans'. It is based on a Yiddish proverb which says 'We plan, God laughs'. That's not to say that God doesn't want us to have plans, doesn't want us to have dreams, but sometimes what we think we want, what we think we will be good at, isn't where our talents and gifts should be directed, for us and for others. Sometimes that realisation comes to us late in life, after pursuing what we think we wanted for years, only to find that no matter how hard we try, no matter how much we sacrifice to make it happen, it isn't actually what we really want to do, it doesn't make us feel complete or fulfilled.

The past fifteen months have made a lot of people rethink their plans, their lives, rethink their priorities, and some have made dramatic changes, leaving high-paid, and high-pressure, jobs to be a delivery driver for a supermarket, or a fruit picker, because they have realised that family is more important than money, time is more important than status. So at the end of July my sister and I will be throwing a few things into a suitcase, without a weight limit, and then throwing a few things we forgot to pack straight into the back of the car, and we'll be heading off to Somerset. Then we'll spend five days doing something, or doing nothing. We'll probably get in a few rambles, of the walking variety, and a few trips out, and the odd afternoon just sitting on the terrace with a coffee, and a few evenings on the patio with a glass of something, and we'll give thanks for what we have, for our holiday, the second choice that is actually the best choice, the right choice, for us, now.

9th July 2021

(A 2–1 victory over Denmark sees the Men's England football team reach its first major tournament final in 55 years!)

Damned if you do, damned if you don't

It was disappointing, but not a surprise, that despite England winning on Wednesday, some pundits and commentators still questioned and criticised the team, and specifically the manager. He should have picked different players, he should have taken this one off, or brought that one on! Win or lose, it seems a football manager is always in for criticism and 'I would have…' comments.

The same applies to our politicians and our church leaders. After weeks, if not months, of lobbying from the hospitality, travel and entertainment industry, supported by opposition MPs, for restrictions to be lifted, for more people to be allowed to meet, to eat and drink together, the proposed lifting of those restrictions has resulted in a few of the same people now saying it's all happening too fast, that staff need to be protected, that venues aren't ready for full capacity. The same clergy who have been questioning the closure of churches, the restrictions on numbers, the ban on communal singing, are now arguing that the church should move slowly, that congregations aren't ready.

Damned if you do, damned if you don't.

I have been reflecting on this with regard to our faith, our Christian living, and our witness, because most of us will have faced the same situation. We will have been criticised or challenged over something we have said or done, or something we haven't said or done, even if our intentions were good, even if what we were trying to do was for the common good, and even if we succeeded.

Jesus tells us, in the Sermon on the Mount, that we should 'Be perfect, therefore, as your heavenly Father is perfect.' It's a big ask, and one that makes me wonder if I am damned if I do, and damned if I don't, try to be perfect as God is perfect, that is. Is it even possible? Jesus himself asked God to take the cup of suffering away from him, he was challenged by the Canaanite woman over his initial refusal to help her daughter, ignoring his own command to love your neighbour. What hope is there for the rest of us? Well, the hope is more than a hope—it is a promise, a promise of love and forgiveness.

God doesn't expect us to be perfect, Jesus didn't expect his disciples to be perfect—if he had, he would have been sadly disappointed. The promise is that if we try, if we really try, then that is good enough for God. We may fail, but if our intentions were good, if our desire to do good, to love one another, is there, and if, when we fail, we acknowledge our failure, then God is forgiving, and understanding, and most importantly loving, and will not damn us, either way.

16th July 2021

(Sunday 11th July saw the final of the Euro 2020 tournament – delayed because of the Covid pandemic. England lost to Italy after a penalty shoot-out)

Did you watch the game?

Football fan or not, the hype and tension of last weekend seemed to permeate into all aspects of our life, but once again, another missed penalty, another missed opportunity! Far from displaying the English virtues of courtesy and respect for others, as extolled by the England coach, Gareth Southgate, some have taken to social media to vilify some players, focusing particularly on Marcus Rashford, who has gone from school meal hero to penalty-taking villain.

But thinking about the reaction of some to the result, and especially to individual players, reminded me of Jesus and the woman accused of adultery – let the one who is without sin cast the first stone. Who amongst us hasn't had a bad day, hasn't said or done something we instantly regretted but couldn't take back, or even just made a genuine mistake in word or action? It is good to remember that the same England coach who took us to the World Cup semi-finals, and the Euros final, is the same man who missed a penalty in the 1996 Euros, against Germany, and was himself vilified. From villain to hero, from hero to villain in the blink of an eye.

Unlike the England players, and celebrities, our mistakes, our bad days rarely—if ever—make it onto social, or unsocial, media. We don't have to relive in printed word or video every aspect of our lives. But sometimes we are our own worst enemy, our own greatest critic. How many times have you made a comment, or made a mistake, and spent hours, days, or even weeks reliving it, going over and over in your head what happened, wondering what those present thought of you, so that the next time you meet them you are a nervous wreck waiting for the inevitable (in your mind) criticism or negative comment—only for them to behave as if nothing happened, because unlike you, they have forgotten all about it.

Would I have wanted to take a penalty for England? – no. Would I have wanted to walk out on Centre Court as the last British singles player? – no. Did I want to be the person who a few weeks ago forgot the Creed at a Sunday service? – no (and I'm sure none of you who were there had the omission playing on your mind as long as I did!).

In his letter to the Thessalonians Paul tells them, 'And we urge you, beloved, to admonish the idlers, encourage the faint-hearted, help the weak, be patient with all of them. See that none of you repays evil for evil, but always seek to do good to one another and to all.'

Be patient with everyone, especially yourselves, we all have bad days, so my prayer each morning is:

'Lord, help me to remember that nothing is going to happen today that you and I can't handle together, and help me not to dwell on my mistakes, on the what-ifs, and the what-might-have-beens.'

27th August 2021

Do unto others...

Sitting down for a relaxing evening we decided to watch the 2015 film adaptation of JB Priestley's *An Inspector Calls*. It took us back to a theatre production we saw many, many years ago where the staging and layout of the theatre made for a very intimate and powerful performance. It was possibly not the right choice for a relaxed evening, because it is a challenging and thought-provoking piece, but at the end it offers a glimmer of hope.

For those who don't know the play, the story centres on the Birlings, a wealthy middle-class family, and the slow revealing, by the mysterious Inspector Goole, of the effect each of them had on the life of a young working-class girl, Eva Smith, leading eventually to her taking her own life. Mr Birling sacked her from his factory because she stood up for workers' rights, Mrs Birling refused her poor relief because she didn't believe the girl's story, Sheila Birling had her sacked from a shop job because she, Sheila, was jealous of her looks and confidence, Eric Birling got her pregnant and Gerald Croft, Sheila's fiancé, cast her off after using her as his mistress. They did all these things because they could.

They had money, position and status, Eva was working class, friendless, and towards the end, desperate.

The play reminds me of the golden rule of Christian faith – 'Do unto others as you would have them do unto you' (Matt 7:12) – and how each member of the family would stand up to Christ's judgement. For Mr and Mrs Birling, and Gerald, the erroneous thought towards the end of the play that they had been had, that it was a hoax, caused them to revert to their old ways, to the belief that they were right, but the hope and inspiration comes from the younger generation, from Sheila and Eric, who feel the full weight and responsibility of their actions and who, we hope, would never treat anyone else in the same way. It may be fiction but it has a message, and it has a challenge.

None of us can know what effect our words and actions can have and we are, thankfully, a long way from the class distinctions of the past, but it is easy to say or do something without realising the effect it has on others. An impatient demand in a shop that adds to the stress of a mother working three jobs, an assumption about asylum seekers or those fleeing persecution, even the simple but important decision as to whether to help a rough sleeper or not, all of these fleeting moments for us impact the lives of people we don't know, and may never see again, but which will affect them for longer than we realise, like a pebble dropped in a pond, the ripples we create continue long after we have forgotten we even dropped it.

So remember, in all you say and do, the golden rule: 'Do unto others, as you would have them do unto you.'

17th September 2021

We're card-carrying, lifelong, members of the union of different kinds

It's starting to get busier in the shop now, with the return of regular familiar faces as well as a steady stream of visitors and tourists. One of the many things I love about being in the bookshop is the fact that you never know who is going to walk through the door, or what they are going to ask, or tell, you, from the random, and impossible, requests – 'I've been recommended a book, it's got God in the title and it's blue, do you know it?' – um, no, we've got a few hundred books with God in the title, and quite a few of them are blue! Or 'I'd like a first edition of the Book of Common Prayer, in modern language' – well, there isn't a modern language version, and a first edition would be, I'm guessing, priceless. To those who just want to look at the building – or do they?

The shop is housed in the oldest church in Chichester, predating the cathedral by about 100 years, and we are the oldest building in Chichester still in use, but more than that, we are still a consecrated place of worship. For almost 1000 years people have been worshipping, praising, and more importantly praying, in our little corner of Chichester, and that continues not only with the annual service to celebrate our patron saint but also with my saying morning prayer every day I'm working, and a soon to be launched evening prayer service.

Many of the people who come to 'look at the building' are actually drawn by the fact it looks like a church and sounds like a church (we have an understated sound system) and so they are delighted to find that we are in fact a church (proving the oft-quoted Duck Test – if it looks like a duck, swims like a duck, and quacks like a duck, then it probably is a duck).

They are drawn because they need something, or want something, but are just not sure what. They are from all Christian denominations and traditions, or none. They tell us stories of great joy – a longed-for child born healthy – of great sadness – loss of a loved one to Covid or cancer – as well as personal stories of their own lives. This week I have met the former head of security at Buckingham Palace who has been diagnosed with cancer and he and his wife wanted books, and support, for healing prayer; a mum who is estranged from her daughter and wanted to just talk to someone without judgement; a grandfather whose grandson was given days to live but is now looking forward to playing football again and wanted to celebrate the news with someone and to buy a holding cross to give support in the weeks ahead; and numerous clergy and ministers with their own stories of parish and personal life with all its ups and downs, joys and struggles.

They say variety is the spice of life, and we certainly get variety in our customers and visitors – all different, all individuals, all unique – but all linked by two facts: firstly, we are all members of the human race, and secondly, we are all loved by God – equally, completely, unquestioningly.

At this point I was going to quote Paul's letter to the Galatians (3:28), 'There is neither Jew nor Greek, there is neither slave nor free, there is neither male nor female; for you are all one in Christ Jesus.' But instead I'd like to direct you to the quote at the beginning of this ramble: 'We're card-carrying, lifelong, members of the union of different   kinds.'
It's from a song of the same name by the Fisherman's Friends, and I think it sums up our Christian faith and how we should live that faith – we are all different but we are all members of that lifelong union that is life, and we live that life in faith, hope and love.

29th October 2021
Ring out those bells tonight!

Don't panic, you haven't missed a couple of months, we're not at Christmas yet, although if you're anything like me, planning and present buying has already started.

On Saturday (30th) church bells across the country, including All Saints East Dean and the Blessed Virgin Mary Singleton, will ring out at 6pm to mark the start of the UN Climate Change Conference (COP26), billed as the most important event on climate change there has ever been, which is why the bells will ring out. They mark the start of the conference, but they are also a reminder that we are all in this together.

Church bells are rooted in our history, and almost everyone lives within range to hear when bells ring out in celebration or when they toll in times of grief or loss. Bells ring to tell of a wedding or the passing of a loved one at a funeral. They call us to worship, or simply let a town, a village, a community know that someone is praying for them. They have been central to the life of this country, and to other countries around the world, for centuries. Church bells have been used to mark the passing of time. In our modern world of clocks, watches, or more likely mobile phones, we are never far from knowing what time it is, even if sometimes we try to ignore that persistent alarm or reminder. However, that hasn't always been the case, and in times gone by, the sound of the church bell set the rhythm of the day, and the times and seasons of our lives. In medieval times, church bells rang out at set times during the day, to tell everyone when prayers were being said, when services were starting, and to mark the start and end of the working day. Labourers in the fields, women working in the home, and travellers on the road could plan their day by listening out for the bells, especially important when unseasonal weather meant the sun didn't seem to rise when it should, or the seasons didn't follow their usual pattern.

But bells have also been used to alert people that something has happened, locally or nationally – an early precursor to the breaking news app, or the WhatsApp group. The ringing of the church bells called people to come together or sent people into hiding. During the Second World War all church bells were silenced, to be rung only in the event of the invasion that so many feared but which thankfully never came. Instead, the bells rang out in celebration of the end of the war, and in the hope of the longed-for peace.

During lockdown, with churches closed and people unable to come together, the bells fell silent again across the country. But as life started to return, as people started to come together again, the ringing of the bells signalled our hope for the future – hope of a return to normality, but also a hope that the lessons we had learnt about the importance of the natural world, about the impact even the smallest of actions can have, will be lessons we will take forward into a new normal – a new way of living together in peace and in kinship with all of God's creation.

The Bishop of Norwich, Graham Usher, the Church of England's lead bishop for the environment, says it so much better than me: "Church bells have traditionally been rung through the centuries to raise the alarm for local communities. The recent 'code red' report from the Intergovernmental Panel on Climate Change (IPCC) is an alarm call for us all. A nationwide 'ring out for climate' on the eve of the COP26 can be a warning symbol, but also one of hope. Hope that this conference will lead to action for us all, like Jesus, to tread more gently on our single island planet home and care more for those already adversely affected by climate change, especially in the economically poorest places on Earth."

So, if you hear the bells on Saturday, or if you see something on the news, remember that they are a call to arms, a call to action, a call to come together – equal in the sight of God, equal in the love of God, but also equally responsible in the eyes of the world for what will happen in the next 10, 20, 50 years.

One of my favourite songs is *From a Distance*, written by Julie Gold. It speaks of what the world looks like from a distance, when we see the bigger picture of what the world **can** be like, if we want it to be.

> *From a distance, there is harmony,*
> *and it echoes through the land.*
> *It's the voice of hope, it's the voice of peace,*
> *it's the voice of every man.*
>
> *From a distance we all have enough,*
> *and no one is in need.*
> *And there are no guns, no bombs, and no disease,*
> *no hungry mouths to feed.*

12th November 2021

This Sunday is Remembrance Sunday, marked as always by Acts of Remembrance up and down the country, and around the world, and the symbol of that remembrance is the Poppy, the bright red flower that flourished amid the destruction, and mud, of the battle fields of Flanders. Colour in the midst of chaos, hope in the midst of despair.

In the past Poppies used to be sold door to door, and in the early 1970s my sister and I would accompany our Mum as she knocked on the doors of the four streets she had been allocated, asking everyone 'Would you like to buy a Poppy?'. Very few said no, and most of those that did, did so because they had already bought one, because at that time both World Wars were still in living memory. Fifty years ago remembering was real people and real places.

We heard the same stories from our neighbours that we heard every year, about where they had fought, or who they had lost, about what had happened to them, and where. Fifty years ago, everyone knew someone who had real and personal memories of the Second World War, on the battle fields or on the home front. Someone who could tell their story, who could keep the memories alive.

But that was fifty years ago, and today the Poppy is a greater symbol of our remembering than it was then, because old soldiers from the Second World War are getting fewer and fewer and we have no one from the First World War left to remember, and to remind us of what we owe them.

On Sunday, in churches and at War Memorials up and down the country, we will hear the names of those who died in the Two World Wars, and as we do so we must remember that behind each name is a person and behind them, a family, a group of friends, a community, a nation that is different because of that one person, that one name.

But remembering is more than just one day of looking back, more than one day of giving thanks for sacrifices made, by those who died and those they left behind. Because right remembering, honourable remembering, means we must also look to the future.

God's ultimate promise for us is that He will dwell with us, that there will be no more mourning, no more crying, no more pain. Wars will end, spears will be beaten into ploughshares, and we will live in peace and in love, because that is what Christ came to offer us, and He died so that we might live.

So how will we remember, rightly and honourably? How will what we do on Sunday, or what we did yesterday, show in how we live our lives next week, next month, next year?

When you take your Poppy off your coat, or out of your hat, think about what you will do with it, and what you will do with the remembering that it symbolises. Perhaps you will put it in a special place from where it will continue to nudge you in your remembering, but whatever you do with it, let it be a symbol of the vision God calls us to take up in our future – individually, as a community, as a nation – that by our living,

We will remember them.

26th November 2021

'Then Joseph got up, took the child and his mother by night, and went to Egypt' (Matt 2:14)

It may seem a little odd to reflect on Mary and Joseph's flight to Egypt when we haven't yet celebrated Jesus' birth, but the deaths this week of the 27 migrants, including 7 women and 3 children, who died trying to cross the Channel, reminded me that the Holy Family had also been forced to leave their homeland and seek refuge in a foreign land.

We'll never know the stories of those who died. We'll never know what prompted their flight from their homelands, and sadly we'll never know what gifts and skills—and in the case of the children, what potential, they would have brought with them. Did that flimsy plastic dinghy contain doctors, scientists, academics? Did the children have the potential to find a cure for cancer, or to be inspirational teachers?

Refugee. Asylum seeker. Economic migrant. Illegal immigrant. These are all very emotive, emotional labels, and how we react to them depends a lot on our upbringing, our life experiences, our political affiliations, and indeed our own socio-economic situation. But the fact is that most of us will have someone in our family, albeit possibly in the distant past, who could lay claim to at least one of those terms.

In *Who Do You Think You Are?* this week, the YouTuber and *Strictly* finalist Joe Sugg discovered that his ancestors had been Huguenot refugees from religious persecution in France, and had sought, and received, asylum in Jersey, in the same way that the Holy Family had sought, and received, asylum in Egypt, fleeing the threat of persecution from King Herod.

Several US presidents have been descended from economic migrants who fled the potato famine in Ireland in the mid-nineteenth century, and hundreds of thousands of Jews fled persecution in Germany as the power of the Nazis took hold.

Two thousand years after Joseph took his family to safety across the Nile, 400 years after the Huguenots began crossing the English Channel, and 80 years after Jews crossed rivers, mountains and seas, religious, political and racial persecution, and economic hardship still force people to leave behind family, friends and what little they own, and face dangerous journeys that we cannot imagine and, as in the case of the 27 migrants, pay the ultimate price for seeking safety, security, and a better life for themselves and their children.

49

So this weekend, as we begin our Advent journey, join me as I pray for the victims, their families, and all those who seek to help refugees and asylum seekers, but especially for those who are working to bring peace to shattered nations, hope to shattered lives, and to resolve the issues which force people to leave their homeland.

3rd December 2021

Hope comes through the door at Christmas

The greatest wish, the greatest prayer, of all clergy, of all congregations, is that our church doors open a lot, especially during the season of Advent and as we celebrate Christmas, the coming of the light of the world. We pray for people to come through our doors because inside we believe they will find what they want, or what they need—Hope, Faith, Joy, Peace, and Love—the theme and focus of our Advent wreaths.

But I have been reflecting on the doors we use, or see, or pass through un-noticing in our preparation for Christmas, during this Advent-tide!

It amazes and delights me every year as to how many people buy Advent calendars, and not just the chocolate ones! Even in our modern technological age, children and adults still want and appreciate the simple things, the simple opening of a cardboard door!

And what about the comings and goings in our own life during Advent, through doors of one shape or size or other. Children, hopefully, going to church for their school carol or Christingle service, then at the end of term the excitement as they rush out of the school gates for the last time before the big day. Older children who have moved away, or are at university, falling exhausted but happy back through the door of childhood homes. Parents proudly taking a gift to their grown-up offspring's new home for the first time, knocking on the door, heralding a new chapter in their family story. Families processing through the doors of rest homes, or occasionally, sadly, into hospitals, to visit parents or grandparents. Those are the door moments to savour!

But sadly, Advent is also the time when people rush through the doors of shops, barely glancing at anyone else, intent on finding the last-minute gift they forgot to buy for their boss or even their loved one! Do we notice the old lady struggling with bags full of food essentials as we let the door swing back on her, or the new mum, unable to control the buggy and the shopping, and scared as to what the future holds, will she cope?

Advent is a time of preparation for Christmas, and Christmas is a time when the lost and the lonely look for somewhere to go, look for a door that will be open to them, to get a warm meal, a friendly face, a smile, maybe a bed for the night, just as Mary and Joseph looked for an open door, a welcoming place to prepare for the birth of their firstborn! And yes, it's a time when refugees and the homeless around the world stand in lines outside pop-up food stations, or huddle up against shop doorways, desperate for some respite from wind and rain, hoping for some human contact that isn't judging or condemning.

Migrants and refugees continue to fill our news feeds and social media. What do the people who get into a small rubber dinghy to cross the busiest shipping lane in the world hope for? The chance of a better life? The chance to educate their children, especially their daughters? The chance to practise their religion, whatever it is, without fear of persecution? Or do they simply hope to be free?

The people of Israel who walked in darkness hoped for light. The angel Gabriel hoped that Mary would say "yes" to God's special invitation. Mary hoped that her fiancé would understand. Joseph hoped he could provide for his family. The shepherds hoped that if they followed the angel's directions, they would see this thing that had taken place. Leaving the comfort of their homes, the Magi hoped that their journey would not be in vain. And watching from a distance, God the Father hoped that someone would pay attention and that this effort to come through the door of heaven to earth as one of us would be worth all the time and trouble.

Life is filled with all kinds of doors of hope and possibility, doors that we need to reflect on during this Advent season, large or small, open or closed, welcoming or foreboding, real or imagined. It is our willingness to open those doors, to walk through them, and then turn and receive with open hearts and open arms all those that come after, that makes our Advent preparation worth it, that makes Christmas a living reality. It's what makes us, as Christians, part of a living faith.

My hope and prayer this Advent is that as we face a still uncertain and sometimes scary future, we may all continue to hope and pray and believe that Love, Peace, Joy and Faith will come through the door of our hearts, our homes and our lives; and that each one of us will have the conviction, compassion and courage to open for others the door that brings heaven to earth, to open the door that gives food to the hungry, drink to the thirsty, and rest to the weary, and hope to the hopeless.

7th January 2022

Sometimes the Church's year can seem a little confusing. It is only 2 weeks ago that we celebrated the birth of Christ on Christmas Day, although I don't know about you but it seems an age ago now, with the decorations packed away for another year, the freezer full of leftover turkey and ham, and the empty chocolate boxes winging their way to recycling. We then moved forward in time last week to welcome the Magi, the Wise Men, at Epiphany, an event that happened up to two years after the birth of the Christ child. And now we jump forward even further and on Sunday celebrate Christ's Baptism in the River Jordan, the start of his public earthly ministry, at the ripe old age of 30! (And to be even more confusing we return to Jesus as a baby at the end of the month when we remember his Presentation in the Temple at Candlemas).

I have to confess I love Baptisms; they are occasions of great joy for the family, the congregation, and the wider community. The start of a new life, be it as a baby, a child, or an adult. They allow us to welcome a new Christian into the family of the world-wide Church, and are sometimes wonderfully and beautifully chaotic!

Some years ago, as a nervous Curate, only a few months after being Ordained Priest, I was asked to baptise a wonderful little girl of 2 ¾, as she proudly told me at our first meeting. As we discussed what would happen at the service, she sat on her mother's lap and listened attentively to everything I said, understanding little but knowing it was important, and knowing it was for, and about, her. So, the big day arrived and I waited outside the Church to welcome her and her family, and all the usual congregation, to the celebration. When they arrived her father nervously took me to one side and said 'sorry, but we may have a problem'. My heart sank – what had happened? As I prepared for the worst he said 'I'm afraid she has a new favourite word, which she is saying all the time! It's No! She doesn't really understand it, but just likes saying it'. Hiding a smile, of relief as much as of amusement, I reassured him that all would be well and ushered them in.

The service progressed as usual until the point of asking the parents and Godparents to stand and confirm their commitment to support their godchild, to pray for her, and to uphold her. As each question was answered a small but determined voice said 'No', with a smile and a giggle. Now some of the family and congregation began to get a little uncomfortable, but we continued and made our way to the font. Being 2 ¾ she refused to be picked up by her parents but instead wanted to stand on a stool and lean over the water of baptism. With a deep breath, and a prayer, I poured the water over her with the words 'I baptise you in the name of the Father...'. Before I could continue the same small, determined voice spoke – Yes! 'and of the Son...' – Yes! 'and of the Holy Spirit...'- Yes!

As we move forward into a new year, with new challenges, new opportunities, I pray that just as with that little girl, we may all say Yes to the God who not only declared that Jesus was His Son, in whom He was well pleased, but has claimed us all as His children. The God who delights in us, who is there for us, who accepts our mistakes, who understands our humanity, and who waits to welcome us with open arms if we will only turn to Him, with a small but determined voice and say 'yes'.

14th January 2022

Prayer – 'the words that someone says or thinks when they are   praying'

The bestselling book of all time is, unsurprisingly, The Bible. It is also the bestselling book in St Olav's, with copies of all different translations flying off the shelves at a joyous rate.

But the second most popular category of book is that on prayer. Whether it is a book of prayers, or a book on how to pray, whether it is a personal account of someone's prayer life or a journal to record your own prayers, prayer has become the new hot topic for the bibliophiles of Chichester and beyond (that's book lovers to you and me).

But why, after 2000 years of Christians being called to prayer, do people now want to find out more? Research has found that the enforced isolation of lockdowns, the enforced separation from our usual daily lives, has meant that a lot of people have turned to prayer, to time with God, who had never done so before, but it also found that many Christians were revisiting their prayer life, were rethinking how, where and what they pray, and they want to find out more. But do we need books to tell us how to pray, should we be trying to emulate the great men and women of old who

58

would spend hours every day in prayer, in conversation and communion with God, or should we find our own way?

The first thing I want to say about prayer is this – whatever you do, and however you do it, just do it! God wants to hear from us, He wants to know we know He is there for us, and whether it is a formal time such as Morning or Evening Prayer, whether it is as part of a daily time of reflection, maybe using a Daily Devotional, whether it is a series of Arrow Prayers as you go about your daily lives, or whether it is the last thing you do before sleep, God doesn't mind. Prayer is important, to us and to God, and it shouldn't be intimidating, or scary, or a chore, it should be personal, comforting, a joy. Maybe we don't always know what to say, but even saying that to God, even admitting we don't know where to start, what to say, what to do, is in itself a prayer, and God is listening.

As we look to the future, as we pray about the future, the Churchwardens and I have decided to suspend, for now, the Monthly Parish Prayer Meeting, so we can revisit, with the help, support, and prayer of the people of the Valley, what we offer, to you and to God, but it is also a chance for us all to think about our own prayers, and our own prayer life. As a priest, I am required to say Morning and Evening Prayer every day, but I am also a great believer in the Arrow Prayer. Those moments during the day when we need a little bit of help, or some comfort, or we wish to give thanks. They can be spoken out loud or simple thoughts. They can be for us, they can be in thanks for our world, or they can be for others, even those we don't know, maybe when we see an ambulance, or see the coastguard helicopter go over. I also use objects to help me pray. I have a Holding Cross, that sits comfortably in the palm of my hand. I use a Rosary, the moving of the beads between my fingers helping me to still my mind and focus my thoughts. I use a lit candle, the light reminding me of Christ's coming as the light of the world.

If you want to find out more about prayer, or to talk about your own prayer life, I am here for you, to support you, and to pray with you, as are other members of the church family, but I also know a really good shop, with friendly helpful staff, who can help you find that book, that holding cross, that rosary, that candle, whatever you need to help you walk with God, to help you talk to God, to help you pray.

60

And finally, if all else fails, if we cannot find the words, then we can do no better than use the words Christ himself gave us:

Our Father, who art in heaven, hallowed be thy name;
thy kingdom come; thy will be done; on earth as it is in
heaven.
Give us this day our daily bread.
And forgive us our trespasses, as we forgive those who
trespass against us.
And lead us not into temptation; but deliver us from evil.
For thine is the kingdom, the power and the glory, for ever
and ever.
Amen.

21st January 2022

When was the last time you were bored? I mean really, truly, mind-numbingly bored? With nothing to do, no TV to watch, no books to read, no mobile to text, no internet to search? The modern world, with all its distractions, the immediate availability of almost everything, means we can fill our time, and our minds, even when we really shouldn't, and be 'busy' 24/7! But is it good for us?

A few years ago, on retreat in the wilds of West Yorkshire, I was told to let myself be bored. I had taken with me a couple of books, some knitting, and of course my mobile phone! If all else failed I could listen to some music, play some games, or surf the net. But no, after we had all settled into our rooms, and had a very welcome cup of tea, the retreat leader sat us down and set out the 'rules' for the week.

v. No mobiles.

v. No internet.

v. No talking (except in our individual sessions with our retreat guide).

v. No distractions.

Specifically, he told us to put away, in our bags or in a drawer, all the things we had brought with us to fill our time. What he wanted us to do was get bored! To have nothing to fill our time, or our minds, nothing to keep our hands busy. But why would the retreat leader, who was also a monk and a priest, tell a group of Christians in search of, yes, a little bit of peace and quiet, but also a close encounter with God, that we should let ourselves be bored? I have written before about giving time to God, about setting aside some time, be it 5 minutes or 30, to just 'be'. Well, what Fr Oswin wanted us to do was more than that. Setting aside time is wonderful, but we still usually have a focus. We might use a daily devotional, or an app, to give us a Bible passage to reflect on. We might be (attempting) to read the Bible in a year. We might use contemplative prayer to empty our minds of all our worries, or a candle to focus our thoughts.

But 'get bored' was a call to not empty our minds but to open them. To allow all the things we bury, all the deep-down worries, insecurities, doubts and fears, to come to the surface, to acknowledge them and to face them. But it is also a time to acknowledge all our blessings, all the good things in our lives that maybe we don't appreciate because we are expected to be striving for more, or because we are expected to be successful and we are expected to be busy. I have to confess that it was hard to 'be bored' and I'm not sure I succeeded, but what my time away from distraction did allow me to do was to let all my deeply buried emotions come to the surface, and to let God in to help me face them. It was a painful process, and in the middle of my week away I hit rock bottom. But as Fr Oswin said, we can only walk towards the light from out of the darkness, and as I sat at the foot of the cross in the grounds of the retreat house, in the pouring rain, I felt Christ looking down at me and telling me He loved me, that all would be well, and that I should trust and wait. Six months later I applied for the post here and the rest, as they say, is history. So getting bored, hitting rock bottom, and letting God in to walk with me was worth it. I trusted, and I waited, and I came here. So next time you reach for the phone, or the book, or the TV remote, to fill your time, why not stop, sit back, and let yourself get bored – who knows where it might lead?

4th February 2022

Sunday 6th February

70th Anniversary of the Accession of Queen Elizabeth II

'I declare before you all that my whole life whether it be long or short shall be devoted to your service and the service of our great imperial family to which we all belong'

Princess Elizabeth 1947

Can there ever have been two more contrasting images. The young Princess Elizabeth looking forward to a bright future on her 21st birthday, and the Queen looking back on a long life, as she sits alone at her husband's funeral.

The Queen dedicated herself to a life of service, to the country and to the Commonwealth, on her 21st birthday and at her coronation only 7 years later Prince Philip swore to be 'her liege man of life and limb', committing himself to a life serving her, and her people, telling his secretary that 'his job first, second and last was never to let her down'.

At the heart of the Queen's service is a strong and committed faith. She has made no secret of that faith and what it means to her. Every Christmas Message refers to it, to the strength she gains from it, even in times of personal and national tragedy. What came as a surprise to some was the strong faith of Prince Philip. He also had to draw on God to guide and support him as he in turn guided and supported the Queen, the family, and indeed the country.

A life of service, a lifetime of putting duty first, and as the Duke of Cambridge put it 'the example and continuity provided by The Queen is not only very rare among leaders but a great source of pride and reassurance' is what has made the Queen a respected, and much loved, figure not just in Britain but around the world.

But she is not alone. There are many people who lead a life of service, locally or nationally, and some are recognised in the Honours list, or with a Lifetime Service Award, but most are not because service is often unseen, personal, and as one RNLI volunteer said – 'it's just what I do, it's who I am'.

Service can be fighting on the front line, it can be putting out to sea in rough weather to save a life, it can be holding the hand of the dying, making a meal for someone, or praying for, and with, the lost, the lonely, or the grieving.

Christ said "'the Son of Man came not to be served but to serve,'" (Matthew 10:45) and we are also called to serve, to put others before ourselves, to work for the common good, not for our own.

So as we remember, and give thanks, for the Queen's lifetime of service this weekend, it is a good opportunity for us all to remember and give thanks for all those who have been of service to us, either personally or nationally, to give thanks for all those who put our needs above their own, even sometimes putting their own lives in danger to save others, and to ask 'what can I do?'

One of my favourite hymns is 'I the Lord of Sea and Sky', often sung at Ordination Services as a rallying call not just to the new priests and deacons but to all people. In the hymn, inspired by Isaiah 6:8 and 1 Samuel 3, God asks who will serve His people, who will be his hands, voice, and heart, and in Princess Elizabeth's declaration in 1947 we can hear the response:

Here I am Lord. Is it I Lord?
I have heard you calling in the night.

I will go Lord, if you lead me.
I will hold your people in my heart.

18th February 2022

Random Act of Kindness Day

Did you know that yesterday (17th February) was the International Random Act of Kindness Day, in the middle of Random Act of Kindness Week? But you may be wondering why we need a day, or a week, dedicated to acts of kindness, shouldn't we be being kind all the time? Well, yes, we should, and most people are, but sometimes we need to be reminded of all the acts of kindness we have received, and also that we ourselves have done, sometimes without knowing the impact it will have. It is also a good time to think of all the times we maybe didn't act, or speak, in the way we should, to be kind, to treat others as we would wish to be treated, to love our neighbour as ourselves.

During lockdown, a lot of people were inspired to perform random acts of kindness for strangers, and that is a very special thing, because it had no return, no reward, for themselves. If we are kind, helpful, to people we know, there is a good chance that that kindness will be returned. If we pay for a friend's coffee because they have forgotten their purse, the next time we meet, they will probably pay for ours. If we help a neighbour whose car has broken down, the chances are they will help us when we need something.

There were so many examples of Lockdown Kindness, but I would like to reflect one. One of our customers in the shop is from Devon, but she now lives and works in Chichester. Her mother, Beryl, however still lives in the village in which she was born. As Covid started to take hold her mother, like so many elderly people, was told to isolate, to not leave her home except to venture out into her small garden for some fresh air. Although her daughter arranged for food to be delivered and phoned her every day, and her local church phoned her once a week, she did start to feel quite lonely and, let's be honest, isolated. About 2 weeks after she had shut herself away there was a knock at the door. Although a little nervous about opening it, she did so only to find there was no one there. Instead, on the doorstep, was a bag containing a bunch of flowers and a tin of biscuits, with an unsigned note 'Enjoy, thought you could do with these'. The bags continued to appear, every 2 to 3 weeks during her isolation, always with a bunch of flowers and a treat, a cake, an Easter egg, or a box of chocolates. To this day she has no idea which of her fellow villagers took the trouble to make sure she knew she was cared for, and to make sure she had something to look forward to. They didn't expect, or indeed want, anything in return, not even a thank you. They did what they did out of kindness and humility, possibly out of gratitude that they themselves were not confined to their home.

There are many examples of, and parables about, acts of kindness in the Bible, but one of the most well-known and often quoted is the story of the Good Samaritan. A stranger helps a man who has been attacked and beaten, left for dead, and ignored by those who should have helped him. The stranger not only stops, not only binds up the man's wounds using valuable oil and cloth but then takes him to an inn and pays for him to be looked after, promising to come back and pay any extra that is needed. It is the ultimate story of random kindness, and of putting another's needs before our own, but it is also a story of kindness leading to kindness. Parables may have been used by Jesus as a teaching aid, to tell his disciples, and us, how we should act, how we should be, but they also call for us to look beyond the story, to think of the thoughts and actions of all those involved. The innkeeper could have turned them away, after all, looking after an injured man would take time and resources. He could have said no because he had no proof that the Samaritan would return as promised, but instead the promise of the parable is that the innkeeper trusted, that he accepted the extra work as his own act of kindness.

In her 1916 book called 'In the Garden of Delight', Lily Hardy Hammond says 'You don't pay love back; you pay it forward'. So, in reflecting on acts of kindness you have received, especially from a stranger, think about how you can pay that kindness, that love, forward. We don't know how Jesus would have continued the story of the Good Samaritan, whether the injured man would have paid his kindness forward, but I do know that Beryl spent her time in isolation knitting hats and booties for the nearest maternity unit as her thank you, as her way of repaying, of paying forward, the act of kindness she had received, in the only way she could.

18th March 2022

Have you ever wondered how birds learn to build nests? It is a question we have been asking in the Rectory as we have watched nests slowly come together in the trees that are in and surround the garden. Well, it may come as no surprise that there have been studies done, where various birds were followed over a number of years to see how their nest building developed. It turns out, that just like us, they learn by trial and error. The researchers found that the first year's nest was a bit of a hit and miss attempt, but that over the years the nests became more stable, more regular in shape, and that the birds dropped fewer twigs and leaves as they made them.

But what impresses me the most, as I watch the birds fly in with twigs often twice their own length, is their perseverance and their patience. They are the epitome of the phrase – if at first you don't succeed, try, try, try again. One pair of magpies began building their nest just before Storm Eunice hit. It was in its early stages and whether they were building their first nest, or whether they hadn't secured it well, the nest was blown away by the winds. Did they give up, did they decide to try something else, or somewhere else? No, they began patiently to rebuild. Twig after twig was carefully woven into the tree to secure it, more twigs were woven in to make the basic shape, and now we watch as they bring moss and leaves in to line the nest and prepare it for the laying and hatching of the next generation.

It reminds me of Thomas Edison and the lightbulb. Edison had over 2000 attempts at inventing the lightbulb before he perfected it. When challenged about his apparent 'failures' he replied 'I didn't fail, I just discovered 2000 ways NOT to make a lightbulb'. Each time it didn't work he honed the technique, he tried new materials, he even went back and started from scratch. Just as the birds with their nests he learnt as he went along, but he didn't give up.

How often do we start a new project, or decide to follow a new diet or fitness regime, but give up when things become too hard, or when things don't go our way, or when it seems we aren't making the progress we had hoped?

Research has shown that most people will give up on a New Years Resolution by the beginning of February. Many people who have given something up for Lent, or taken something on, last until about the third week, and then either forget, or life gets in the way, or they are just too tired, or busy, to keep going and then decide that as they have given in, or failed, once, there is no point in keeping going, no point in starting again.

I bought a new Bible just before Christmas – The Bible in One Year. Every day there is a Psalm or a section from Proverbs, an Old Testament reading and a New Testament Reading. I committed to reading the Bible in a year, on top of the readings at Morning and Evening Prayer. To put it into context, in following the daily readings set by the Church of England Lectionary, it takes 3 years to read the whole Bible, and even then, some passages are left out. But I was determined and every evening I read the chapters set, made notes or highlighted passages that resonated, and prayed. But then one night, at the end of a busy week, I was so tired that I just couldn't even pick it up, let alone concentrate on what I was supposed to be reading, so I missed a day. The next day when I opened the Bible my heart sank at the thought of having to read 2 days' worth in one go, so I again put it down and reached for an Agatha Christie instead.

I felt guilty, and a bit of a failure, that I had not only let myself down, but also God, and was on the point of giving up, of putting the Bible at the back of the shelf where I couldn't see it, and trying to forget I had ever started. But then I remembered good old St Peter, my favourite Apostle and Saint. On the night before Jesus died, Peter declared in front of all the disciples that he would never deny Him, that even if he had to die with Jesus, he would not leave him!

Well, we all know what happened next. As Jesus is brought before the High Priest, Peter is challenged three times as to whether he is one of Jesus' followers, and three times he denies it. Three times the man who Jesus trusted turned his back on him and walked away. Peter failed him, Peter let himself down, let the other disciples down, and let God down. But Jesus forgave him, and more than that Jesus declared Peter the Rock on which he would build His Church.

Jesus understood, understands, the frailty of human nature, that we, like Peter, will commit ourselves to follow Him absolutely, to pray every day, to read the Bible in a year, to sacrifice our time for others, but that sometimes we will fail, that events will get in the way, that other people will get in the way, and that we may end up doubting ourselves. If we can't do this, or that, if we can't finish what we started, if we can't be perfect at the first attempt we may as well just give up!

That was how I felt, I wanted to give up my new Bible because I knew I could never catch up on the days I had missed, but then just like the birds with their nests, just like Edison with his lightbulb, I decided to persevere, to learn from the past and to be realistic in my expectations of myself.

I still haven't caught up where I should be, because I have missed a few more days over the past couple of weeks and so I won't read the Bible in a year, it will probably take me until next Easter, but I will finish it, and I will thank God when I do for helping me see that it's OK to not be perfect, to sometimes have to accept that life and circumstances get in the way, and to just regroup, refocus, and persevere.

So if you feel tempted to give up on prayer, because you don't do it every day, or don't know if you are doing it 'right', or are tempted to give up on your Lenten promise because occasionally it is just too hard, remember St Peter, remember the birds, and remember Edison, and accept, and give thanks, that God is not after perfection at the first attempt, or the second, or the third, He just asks us to turn up, to turn to Him, to give the best we can, as we are, who we are, and He will always, always, love us for it.

1st April 2022

I have too much stuff! There, I've admitted it. I have too many books, I have too many clothes, I have too many nick knacks, I just have too much stuff!

As a family we were never really into the Great Spring Clean. Some of my friends used to spend a whole weekend moving all the furniture, where possible, out of every room, cleaning the whole room, and then putting the furniture, and everything else, back into the room, deciding what to keep and what to get rid of, as they went. It was a great idea and incredibly therapeutic, and I loved going round and helping out, for a few hours, but there was one problem with the Manouch family trying it – we had too much stuff!

Last year I wrote about my great wardrobe switch over, when the summer clothes went away and the winter ones came out, and how many clothes I got rid of in the process. I tried to do the reverse on Thursday, although as it started to snow just as I opened the wardrobes and the temperature plummeted as I tried on summer dresses and cropped trousers, they have gone back into the spare bedroom, and the winter clothes have remained in the wardrobe. I have got rid of a couple of sacks to the charity shop, and I know that when I do finish the great switch over my wardrobe doors will shut, for a while, and my shoes will fit on the rack, for a while, until I buy more!

But what about the rest of the house? It's amazing how much stuff you can accumulate over a very short period of time. When my sister moved up to Singleton last year, we had to merge the contents of two households! Now in most of the rooms it worked fine, the Rectory has more, and bigger, rooms than we had before and so we needed all of the furniture and found room for all the pictures, and most of the nick knacks, but in the kitchen our cupboards were full to overflowing. So, after the great clothing sort out, we turned our attention to the pots and pans, the storage boxes and the baking trays! 8 saucepans are now down to 5, after all, we only have 4 hobs! There is only so much space in a freezer for the results of bulk cooking, so some of the plastic boxes had to go! We tried, as best we could, to declutter the kitchen, and to put things in the best place for ease of access and frequency of use!

On the next wet, cold, windy Thursday when we can't garden, we will tackle the office, putting things where they should be, and getting rid of the surplus, and I will rely on my sister to ask the question 'are you ever going to read that book again?' because although I can part with a dress or a saucepan with ease, books are a different matter!

But what about decluttering our lives and our minds? Lent is traditionally a time of sacrifice, of repentance, of reflection, but it is also a time of cleansing, of throwing off some of what the world has cluttered our minds and lives with, of deciding what is important to us in terms of our faith, in terms of our relationships, and in terms of who we are, who we are called to be.

In our New Testament reading this Sunday (Philippians 3: 4b – 14), Paul writes to the Philippians of who he was, 'a Hebrew born of Hebrews; as to the law, a Pharisee; ..as to righteousness under the law, blameless' and then goes on to tell them that all of his credentials, all of what made him a zealous persecutor of the followers of Jesus, The Way, he regards as loss, because of the love of Christ Jesus, and that he sees all he was in the past as 'rubbish'.

It is a hard thing to look at who we are, what we have, and decide it is rubbish, and it must have been hard for some of the people of Philippi to hear Paul tell them that after all he had been through, he still did not believe he had reached his goal of 'gaining Christ and being found in him', but instead was still pressing on to know Jesus, to understand Jesus, and

80

to love Jesus. If Paul hadn't reached his goal, after all he had done and suffered, then what chance was there for them, for us?

I found it quite easy to throw out clothes I no longer wanted, or which no longer suited me, or suited who I am, where I am. It was quite easy to get rid of pots and pans we no longer needed and although it will be tough, I will get rid of books I no longer need, or want. It is harder to throw out our fears, our doubts, our questions. It is harder to decide what we have, what we do, that prevents us opening ourselves fully to the love of Christ, and that prevents us taking that love out into the world, and to decide to throw it away, to sometimes turn our backs on our past and embrace a new future.

I pray that I, and you all, may be like Paul, and 'press on towards the goal, for the prize of the heavenly call of God in Christ Jesus', because that is a prize worth fighting for, a prize worth 'forgetting what lies behind and straining forwards to what lies ahead' as we turn our thoughts towards Holy Week and to the Greatest Day - Easter Sunday.

8th April 2022 – Palm Sunday

Have you ever been somewhere that you have always wanted to go, but then been disappointed when you got there? We went to Egypt many years ago on a cruise and took a trip out to the Pyramids. I had always wanted to see them, and to see the Sphinx, but when we arrived, they were not what I had hoped for. Yes, they are amazing and awesome, but they are no longer surrounded by desert as far as the eye can see; Cairo is approaching them rapidly. We were surrounded by people trying to sell us something, the guides and tour leaders carried guns, and even the police were on the make. The Sphinx was surrounded by hoarding, and although we went inside and climbed up to see the face, it didn't have the majesty I had hoped for.

I had the same slight sense of disappointment with some of the places we visited on a Pilgrimage to the Holy Land. We visited Bethlehem, no longer the small, insignificant village it was in Jesus' time, but now a bustling tourist destination. It is full of souvenir shops, hotels, and restaurants. But then we went to the sight traditionally believed to be where the angels appeared to the shepherds. Yes, it is also a little bit touristy, with a large chapel, souvenir stalls, and coffee shops, but if you go down into one of the outdoor chapels, simply furnished with benches and a small wooden altar, it is a place of peace, of tranquillity, and a truly Holy Place. There may have been a couple of thousand people milling around only a few feet above us, but where we were, there was wonderful silence, broken only by the sound of children in a school across the valley, and the sheep in the field next door.

I was reminded of my visit to Jerusalem today when I joined in the Palm Sunday (on Friday) procession with the children of West Dean School. Led by Tilly the Shetland Pony, who stood in wonderfully for the donkey, we walked along part of Centurion Way, around the school field, and back to the playground, singing, shaking maracas, and waving palm branches. Once gathered together again, I blessed their Easter Garden, beautifully created by the children in a wheelbarrow. Although our Church Easter Garden will represent the opening of the tomb, the children had surrounded theirs with a wicker fence, made from ice-lolly sticks, with The Garden of Gethsemane written on them. The Garden at the foot of the Mount of Olives, where Jesus was arrested, and a garden that we visited as part of our tour of Jerusalem.

Jerusalem was in some ways as disappointing as the Pyramids. There is, in many of the chapels and churches, a lot of bling, and also a lot of people. We queued for almost an hour to enter the Church of the Holy Sepulchre, the traditional site of the crucifixion, only to be hurried through once inside, with little time to see anything, and certainly no time to pray. We then made our way to the top of the Mount of Olives and walked down a very steep and very rocky path through the olive groves and past the massive cemeteries, both Jewish and Christian, on either side. When we reached the bottom, we again joined a queue to go into the church, and I have to confess that by this time, many of us were hot, tired, and ready to return to the hotel.

But then it hit me, we were standing in the Garden of Gethsemane. The actual place where Jesus had gone to pray many times when he visited the city, and the place where Judas had betrayed him. Was the church built on the actual spot of the fateful kiss? Who knows, but at that moment it didn't matter, because the garden, full of trees that some believe had been there for over 2000 years, was the garden where Jesus had walked, knelt, and prayed. Some of us left our place in the queue to stand to one side, to take in where we were, and to put the bling, the hype, and the noise out of our minds, and to just be. It was a wonderful moment, it was what we had gone for, and it made the whole trip worthwhile.

On Sunday, we begin Holy Week. At Singleton, we will celebrate Palm Sunday, the joyful entry of Jesus into Jerusalem riding humbly on a donkey. On Wednesday, at the last of the Lent Suppers, we will look at Mary Magdalene, the first person to see the Risen Christ. On Maundy Thursday, our service at East Dean will remember the first ever Last Supper, and Jesus' New Commandment to love one another as he has loved us. Good Friday is a time of prayer and reflection, with the opportunity to come and pray in Singleton, for however long you wish, between 12 and 3, the Hours of Agony for Jesus on the cross. Holy Saturday is a day of waiting, of anticipation, ready for the Greatest Day, when on Easter Sunday, at West Dean, we get to shout with joy, 'He is Risen'.

I pray that your Holy Week will be blessed, that along with all the plans for joyful family gatherings, all the shopping for cards, and Easter Eggs, along with all the busyness of school holidays or trying to get everything done ready for the long weekend, you will find, as I did standing at the foot of the Mount of Olives, that moment to just be, to reflect on what happened over 2000 years ago, and to be ready on Easter Day to shout with joy, and hope, and excited expectation 'He is Risen, Alleluia, Alleluia, He is risen indeed.'

22nd April 2022

I love a good parade, especially a military one. It is what we Brits do best, pomp and circumstance. This Saturday (23rd April 2022), there is a parade in Chichester. The Royal Sussex Regimental Association, led by the band of the Princess of Wales Royal Regiment, will parade from Priory Park to the Cathedral, offering the salute to the Mayor as they go.

Once at the Cathedral, they, together with their guests, including my sister and me, will be part of the St George's Day service, which will include the rededication of the Regimental Chapel. The chapel was originally dedicated to the memory of the men from the Regiment who died during The Great War, the War to end all Wars! It was a place for the families of the fallen to gather for quiet contemplation, and to find their relative's name amongst the 7302 inscribed on the panels affixed to the walls.

Of course, it wasn't the War, the end all Wars, and after the Second World War, a Book of Remembrance was added, listing all the men of the county regiment who have died in active service since 1939, including our uncle, until it was amalgamated with other regiments to become The Queen's Regiment (West Sussex). In 1992, it was amalgamated again, this time with the Royal Hampshire Regiment, to form the Princess of Wales Royal Regiment, and again they paraded through the streets of Chichester to their chapel.

In 1914, an Army Chaplain wrote to the family of a soldier who had died soon after the war began and said, "Tell the Territorials and soldiers at home that they must know God before they come to the front if they would face what lies before them. We have no atheists in the trenches. Men are not ashamed to say that, though they never prayed before, they pray now with all their hearts."

There are no atheists in the trenches has sometimes been used as a derogatory term, used to suggest that those of no faith have tried to 'jump on the bandwagon' when faced with danger, that somehow their prayers are less than those of long-standing faith, that somehow God will judge them differently. A Christian newspaper even used a version as a headline recently, 'There are no Atheists in Ukraine'. I have to admit I wanted to throw all of the copies I found in the bin, because to suggest that the people of Ukraine, a deeply faithful people, be they Christian, Muslim or Jewish, were turning to God, turning to prayer, only now because of the horrendous, terrifying war is an insult to them, an insult to their faith, be it long held or newly found, and it is an insult to God.

I am always humbled when visitors to the shop, or people I met as a Day Chaplain at the Cathedral, or people I meet out and about, begin by telling me that they don't believe in God, or that they don't go to church, but then either ask for prayer, or accept with gratitude my offer to pray with them, or for them. The God I believe in welcomes all prayer, welcomes all people, whether they are the prayers offered after a lifetime of faith, or prayers offered for the first time, whether they are prayers offered in fear, prayers offered in times of need, or prayers offered in joyful thanks.

I have no doubt that at the service in the Cathedral tomorrow we will not only remember and pray for those who lost their lives in conflicts past, but also for those who are currently fighting, and dying, for their homeland, for freedom, be it in Ukraine, or in the 22 other wars currently ongoing around the world, and also for those from this country and others who have joined with them in that fight.

'No one has greater love than this, to lay down one's life for one's friends.' (John 15:13)

To God, all lives are precious, all people are His children, and all are loved.

88

13th May 2022

I am an occasional watcher of Gardeners' World, occasional not because the tv isn't switched on, but because I find that Monty Don's voice very successfully sends me to sleep, if he made relaxation tapes, the insomniacs of the world would snap them up! But when I do stay awake long enough to find out what my sister may be inspired to do next in the garden, I am often confused by the names of the plants. The presenter will be extolling the virtues of Digitalis purpurea, and I'm thinking, 'wow, that sounds exotic', and then the camera pans to show the plant in question, and then it's 'oh, it's a foxglove!'. I don't know why they have started using the scientific name for all the plants rather than the common name, but as an inexperienced and not very knowledgeable gardener, I find it mystifying and a little intimidating.

But it did get me thinking about words and names, why we use them, and what they mean.

Driving home from work the other day, we were looking at the sheep in the fields, and it got me wondering why we have a herd of cows, but a flock of sheep, and not a flock of sheeps! Why is it a cow in the field, but beef at the table? Well, the former goes back to Old English, and the latter goes all the way back to the Norman Conquest, when the lower classes, the native Anglo-Saxon farmers, were responsible for the day-to-day work of raising the livestock, the cows and the pigs, which would then be gastronomically transformed to grace the table of the wealthy Norman lords who brought with them the French words for the cooked meat, so cow became beef, and pig became pork.

Then I began to think about the English language in general. I am always humbled by those who can learn a second language, because despite years of trying at school, and since, I cannot get to grips with French or German, and have had to admit defeat, I just don't have an ear for languages. But my greatest admiration goes to all those who learn English as their second language, because it isn't easy, and even native speakers get tripped up by our different spellings and pronunciations. Locally, we have Bosham and Cosham. In looking at them, they should be pronounced the same, but they aren't, and don't even get me started on the differences between there, their, and they're!

We then have the words that have changed in meaning over time. In the Book of Common Prayer, we pray that all in authority will 'truly and indifferently minister justice' but I, and many of my clergy colleagues, change it to say 'truly and impartially', because in 1662 that is what indifferently meant, to be fair, to be impartial, to treat everyone the same, with no difference between rich or poor, man or woman, but to 21st century ears indifferently means to be disinterested, to not care, and I want those in authority to care, to be interested.

Names and words can have so many different meanings, and can be meant one way by the person saying it, but understood a different way by the person hearing it. Even worse is an email or a text, or a Facebook or twitter post, which without the benefit of hearing how something is said, in jest with a smile, or in anger with a frown, can lead to confusion and sometimes real hurt. I was once advised that I should think once before saying something, think twice before writing something, and think three times before posting something on social media, and it is good advice that I mostly stick to.

The bible is not immune to the misunderstandings of language, or to personal interpretation. St Paul is a great one for being misunderstood or misused. In many of his epistles, or letters, he can come across as misogynistic and controlling, but he is responding to particular situations in particular communities, and we don't have the other half of the correspondence to inform our understanding. But every so often, we get to know the real Paul, and we get the real message he is sending to the Christian communities he is serving and supporting, and to us. In his letter to the Galatians (3:28) he has a simple but important lesson for the diverse community of faith there, and for the generations who were to follow, 'There is no longer Jew or Greek, there is no longer slave or free, there is no longer male and female; for all of you are one in Christ Jesus.' There is no one better than anyone else, no one more important than anyone else, in the sight of God, and in the love of God.

This Sunday in our Gospel reading, we will hear once again of The New Commandment that Jesus gave to his disciples, and to us, 'Love one another as I have loved you'. It was only a few weeks ago that I reflected on what it is to love and serve, to follow the New Commandment, but as we all watch the events in Ukraine, and in the other war zones around the world, it is a message we all need to hear, that we are loved, and a message we all need to take to heart in how we treat others, to love them as Jesus loved us. There is no confusion in what Jesus says, no possibility of misunderstanding, there can be no question as to what the message, what the promise is, of the death and resurrection of Jesus. Jesus loved, loves, everyone equally, impartially, and offers that love to all. All we have to do is do the same.

27th May 2022

How many times have you seen or heard 'It's a once in a lifetime opportunity to…'? A once in a lifetime opportunity to buy this house or that car. It's a once in a lifetime opportunity to see this event, or to travel to that place? I have to admit that my more cynical head often reacts to these statements or offers with a shrug of the shoulders and a 'Really?'. Afterall, houses come up for sale pretty often, cars change hands quite regularly, and if you have the time and the money, then travelling anywhere in the world isn't really a once in a lifetime event anymore. Even space travel is now available to anyone, if they can afford it. But sometimes events can truly be described as 'Once in a lifetime'.

Next weekend's Platinum Jubilee is one such event. It is, in fact, likely to not only be a once in a lifetime event for everyone alive today, from babes in arms to the many centenarians around today (no, I didn't know that was what someone over 100 was called either), but a once only event ever. For 70 years, since the age of 26, the Queen has had one job, with no opportunity to change career, to move company, or even to retire. At the age of 21, she dedicated her life to the service of the people, the country, and the commonwealth, a dedication she reaffirmed at her coronation. And it is a life of service that has been sustained and strengthened by her faith, and by the faith of those closest to her.

As the country and the commonwealth, and many others around the world, come together next weekend to give thanks for a lifetime of service, you will be able to tell your children, or your grandchildren, that you did see and experience a truly 'once in a lifetime event'.

Of course, history does show us that once in a lifetime events do happen, and more often than we may have thought. From events to celebrate, such as the first man to land on the moon or the fall of the Berlin Wall, to events that horrify us, and horrified many of those who experienced them, such as the dropping of the first atomic bombs on Hiroshima and Nagasaki. Some once in a lifetime events are ones that we hope and pray will be an 'It only happened once' event, while others we hope will be repeated in one form or another for future generations to enjoy and celebrate.

The Christian faith is built on an 'It only happened once' event, but it is an event that is not only remembered and celebrated every Sunday, but an event that forms the bedrock to all we believe, and a beacon of light and hope for our future, and the future of the world. Jesus' Resurrection, his

94

overcoming of death and the promise of eternal life that it brought, was an event witnessed by very few people, in the grand scheme of things, but it, and the events that followed over the next 50 days, gave his disciples the strength, the courage, and most importantly the faith, to take Jesus' message out into what was often a hostile and unforgiving world.

The Gospels tell of many post resurrection appearances of Jesus to his disciples and followers, and they can, I admit, sometimes seem confusing and even contradictory. Did he first appear to Mary Magdalene alone, or was she with the other women? Did he meet the disciples in the Upper Room, or on the shore of the Sea of Galilee? Did he break bread with the men at Emmaus before or after meeting Peter? As is so often the case, the Gospel accounts are directed at a particular group of listeners, and so emphasize what they can relate to, in much the same way newspapers today can report the same event in 100 different ways.

What we do know is that after being seen by up to 500 people, Jesus returned to his Father in heaven on Ascension Day. Although Ascension Day was actually yesterday (Thursday 26th), 40 days after Easter, we will be celebrating it this Sunday at East Dean, marking the end of Jesus' human earthly ministry, the last time he was seen in human form. But this next 'it only happened once' event in the life of the Jesus, and in the life of the growing faith community that believed in him and embraced his teaching and his commandments, was followed very quickly by a new event that we celebrate next weekend, Pentecost.

As Jesus prepared to return to his Father, he told those waiting on the mountaintop that he would send them a helper, that he was not sending them out alone to spread the Good News of the Kingdom of God, and that helper would be God's Holy Spirit, the third in the Holy Trinity of Father, Son and Holy Spirit. But unlike the Resurrection, unlike the Ascension, the gift of the Holy Spirit was not, and is not, a once only event. It isn't even a once in a lifetime event. We pray for the gift of the Holy Spirit every time we remember the events of the Last Supper at the Eucharist, or in home communions. We pray for the gift of the Holy Spirit at Baptisms, Confirmations, Ordinations, and Coronations. We pray for the gift of the Holy Spirit at Weddings and Funerals, and we pray for the gift of the Holy Spirit in times of joy and in times of sadness.

As we prepare to celebrate Ascension, Pentecost, and the Platinum Jubilee, we pray for the gift of the Holy Spirit on the people of Ukraine, and Russia, and on all who are suffering at this time, and especially we pray for the gift of the Holy Spirit on the families and friends of the children and teachers killed in the Elementary School in Uvalde, Texas on Tuesday.

3rd June 2022

One of the commentators at yesterday's Trooping the Colour said that the Queen's smile can light up a room. Today, that smile is lighting up the whole world as it is seen in newspapers, on TV, and on social media across the Commonwealth, and beyond. But in 1953, another Queen's smile, and her joy, lit up post war Britain and also travelled round the world.

On 2nd June 1953, 10.4 million people in the UK watched the coronation on TV, often with whole streets crowding into one house, to watch the event on a small black and white set. 1.5 million watched the great event in pubs and cinemas, and 11 million people listened on the radio. It was a truly joyful occasion, giving the country a much-needed lift after the Second World War, but there was one person who embodied the joy of the occasion more than any other, and that person was Queen Salote of Tonga.

As the procession left Westminster Abbey after the service, the great British weather did its best to spoil the day. The skies opened, and the temperature dropped. Umbrellas went up, waterproof capes were put on, and carriages stopped to have their covers put up, but not the carriage carrying Queen Salote and Sultan Ibrahim IV of Kelantan. Despite the fact that she was wearing traditional Tongan dress, a coconut fibre skirt and a satin rose-coloured mantle, neither of which was designed for wet weather, she insisted the carriage roof stay down. She wanted to enjoy the occasion, she wanted to see the people enjoying the occasion, and she wanted to honour her friend, Queen Elizabeth. But the reason people remember Queen Salote isn't simply because she kept her carriage uncovered, no, the reason the people who were there, and the millions watching on TV, took her to their hearts was because she never stopped smiling. As the Sultan got wetter and wetter, and sank in his seat, Queen Salote appeared not to feel the rain or the cold. Throughout the whole procession, she sat upright, waved, and smiled. Even to this day, if you ask anyone who saw the coronation, they will remember the Queen of Tonga, they will remember her smile, and they will remember that they smiled with her.

This weekend, there will be, I hope, a lot of smiling. There will be, if the amount of alcohol leaving the supermarkets is anything to go by, a lot of parties, and those parties will not only celebrate the amazing 70-year reign of Queen Elizabeth, but probably also the fact that this is the first time in almost 2 ½ years that we are able to really come together in joy, in hope, and in love, to meet with family and friends, and to celebrate all that we have with those that we love.

99

But this weekend, we are not only celebrating the Platinum Jubilee, but as a church and a people of faith, we are celebrating Pentecost, the great joyful celebration of the coming of the Holy Spirit. Just as in 1953 when the people of Britain were still recovering from the Second World War, just as now when we are still recovering from the pandemic, and facing a challenging future, Jesus' disciples were recovering from the anguish of the Crucifixion, which had been replaced by the joy of the Resurrection, and then despair as they saw Jesus once again leave them as he ascended to His Father in heaven. They didn't know what the future held; they only knew that Jesus had promised them a helper and a comforter.

The coming of the Holy Spirit filled the disciples with joy, and that joy was infectious, just as the joy and the smile of our Queen is infectious, and just as the joy and the smile of Queen Salote was infectious. We are all facing challenges and uncertainties at this time, some financial, some physical, some emotional, and it can sometimes feel overwhelming, but just as the Queen found joy despite the pain, just as Queen Salote found joy despite the rain, I pray that you may also find joy in the smile of a loved one, in the company of friends, and in the knowledge that we have God with us through all the trials of life, and I pray that in all you do,

100

through the tears and the joy, you will have the gift of the Holy Spirit, your helper and comforter.

Gracious God, we give you thanks for the reign of your servant Elizabeth, our Queen, and for the example of loving and faithful service which she has shown among us. Help us to follow her example of dedication and to commit our lives to you and to one another, through Jesus Christ our Lord. Amen.

24th June 2022

'I can see clearly now the rain is gone', so wrote Jimmy Cliff, but perhaps I should change the words to 'I can see clearly now the scratches are gone!'

This week I collected new glasses and new contact lenses from the optician, and I must admit I hadn't realised quite how scratched and battered my old glasses were! Of course, our eyes are amazing things, and they have compensated for the scratches and the finger marks, but wow, what a difference to have completely clear and clean lenses! I also hadn't realised how much my sight had changed over the past few years until I put on the new specs and everything was clear, bright, and most importantly, in focus. My new contact lenses will also mean, I hope, that I will no longer have momentary pauses in the middle of Sunday worship as I try to refocus on the small print of the service book!

It's said that the eyes are the window to the soul, and it's true that we can often understand how someone is feeling not from what they say, or how they act, or even if they are smiling, but from looking them in the eye. But how we see others is also a window into our own souls.

On the day I visited the optician, the bible reading for my morning prayer was about just that, how we see others and how we treat others. In Matthew's Gospel (Ch 7, verses 1 – 5), Jesus tells us that we should not judge others because we will also be judged by the same standard. He tells his disciples, and us, that we shouldn't look at the speck of sawdust, the apparent faults or failings, in our neighbour's eye, and ignore the plank in our own! We have the same faults, the same failings, the same issues, but it is so often easier to either criticise others or to judge them, without seeing or acknowledging what we ourselves do that is unkind, or ungracious, a sin against them, against ourselves, and against God.

There is a famous quote, 'Before you judge a man, walk a mile in his shoes,' which reminds us that we can never know what someone else is going through simply by looking at their lives from a distance. We can look at the outward appearance, the house, the car, the lifestyle, and think they are successful, we can see them laughing and smiling and think they are happy and content, but it may be that they are 'keeping up appearances', that they are covering up pain, stress, or a sense of loss or failure.

In the early 1990's, when the mortgage rate was at 15%, inflation hit 7%, and there were over 3 million unemployed, a new curate arrived in a small-town parish. They were young, fresh faced, and straight out of theological college. The town seemed, on the surface, to be affluent, and so when the Vicar, older, wiser, and more experienced, asked them to write a report on the state of the parish, the young curate jumped at the chance. They set off in their new car, a gift from their parents, and toured around the streets looking at the houses. They then wrote their report. The opening line said 'There is no poverty or need in the parish'. The Vicar only read that line before putting the curate in their car and driving to the outskirts of the town. As they stood looking down the road, the Vicar pointed to various houses and told the curate of the father who had lost his job, the parents who went to bed hungry so their children could eat, and the mother working 3 jobs. He also told them of the neighbours who left food parcels on doorsteps, who offered sleep overs with their own children to ease the pressure, who drove out of their way to give lifts. The curate stopped looking at the houses, at the outside, and started looking at the people. They stopped judging from their own perspective and started judging from God's. They then rewrote the report, which began 'There are areas of great need in the parish, but also of great love'.

As we look at our world today, still recovering from the pandemic but now faced with wars, natural disasters, and poverty, we also see areas of great need and we are called to show love, to offer support, looking with eyes that see beyond the outward appearance, that see beyond the scratches, that focus through the clean and clear lens of love. We may not be able to walk in the shoes of a refugee, or of the homeless, or of the Afghans hit by the earthquake, but we can walk with them in love, with our eyes and our hearts, open.

1st July 2022

One of the joys, and also the challenges, of keeping a journal is looking back. It's picking up a journal from 5, 10, or even 14 years ago and seeing what was exciting me, what was troubling me, and what was going on in the world at the time. It is also a real eye opener as to how I, and my life, have changed over that time.

I began my first journal in 2008 when I was made redundant after 25 years in the pension industry. Although it was a shock when it happened, because it was unexpected, I admit I woke up the next day with a smile on my face and the feeling that a great weight had been lifted, because deep down I knew that I was being called by God to do something different, but at that stage I didn't know what. I also felt just a little bit grateful that I wasn't going to have to take the slightly scary decision to hand in my notice and step out into the who knew what, because the decision had been taken for me.

A few days after I was told of the redundancy, my sister gave me my first journal to help me focus my thoughts, to help me work through my anxieties and fears for the future, and also to reflect on what God wanted from me next. I now have some 20 or so completed journals on a shelf in my bedroom.

They are in all shapes and sizes, some brightly coloured and some leatherbound, because every Christmas since 2008, I have received a new journal, and in some years when I wrote an awful lot, I also got one for my birthday.

Every day, however busy I was, whatever else was going on, I would find time to write, to reflect, and to record my thoughts and my prayers. And then came Lockdown. Like so many people, overnight my life went from being extremely busy, out at work, or on parish duty down in Wittering, to being stuck at home, with a phone, a zoom connection, and with one walk a day. At first, my journaling continued, after all, there was a lot to reflect on, and then as life slowed down, as we, like most people, got into a new routine, I began to not write every day, and then it became a once a week catch up activity.

I'm slowly getting back into the habit of daily writing and reflecting, and looking back over past journals, rereading what was happening to me and to the world, has given me the incentive to start again. Because when I look back, I realise that much of what I feared, much of what seemed insurmountable problems, either didn't happen, or were in fact an opportunity to grow and develop. When I look back at the early journals, I see uncertainty and nervousness for the future, but now, sitting in the Rectory office and looking forward to the future, those uncertainties were unfounded, and the nervousness as to what I would do, and would I be good enough, and even was it truly God's call I was feeling, is no longer there.

My old journals remind me that we cannot know the future, but we can accept the present and look forward, looking at the bigger picture and the wider world. They are also a reminder that we may not think we have an answer to our prayers, but often the answer is there, and not what we expected. 14 years ago, I prayed for guidance as to what I should do next, and through my redundancy, I was able to take the time to step back and to reflect, and to be open to God's will for me. It is also a reminder that when we pray, we have to acknowledge that God doesn't work to our timetable, nor to our wants, and that we need to accept that our prayers may not be answered now, but in the future, or that in fact, what we wanted was not what we needed.

8th July 2022

Do you ever arrive somewhere, either walking or in the car, and think, I don't remember that journey. Did I stop at the traffic lights or the junction? Did I look before I crossed the road? It's quite disconcerting and sometimes a little scary, but all I can do is hope and pray that if something needed me to react, then I would do so.

But there are also times when we don't see what is going on around us because we are engrossed in our phones or laptops. My sister loves travelling on the bus to work because, being a little higher up than in a car, she can look over the hedgerows and see the sheep in the fields, or the crops growing, but very few other people are looking out of the window; they are texting or watching YouTube videos. And then there are the people walking through town with their heads down, earphones in, totally oblivious to the world around them. I must admit that on Wednesday, I got a little frustrated at the number of people who, because they were on their phones, seemed to have lost the ability to walk in a straight line! Coupled with the number of market stalls set up in Chichester, it made for a very 'interesting' lunchtime outing. One poor lad even walked straight into the tables set up outside Bill's and would have gone over head first if someone hadn't caught him.

A few years ago, before the advent of working from home, I had to travel up to London on what was then a very busy commuter train. I managed to get the last window seat in the carriage and settled down for the journey. Around me, every table and dropdown shelf was covered with laptops and phones, and no one even looked up when someone sat down next to them. At the next station, a young man got on who I will call Ben. Because a few people had gotten off, he managed to get a seat opposite me, but on the aisle. Next to him was another young man, about the same age, who was totally engrossed in his work. After a couple of minutes, Ben tapped him on the arm and asked if they could swap seats. After getting over the shock of someone breaking the unwritten rule of not speaking on public transport, he asked why? 'Well,' said Ben, 'I want to look out at the countryside and you want to work, so can we swap?' After much huffing and puffing, the man agreed, and they swapped seats.

As we approached Arundel, Ben looked at me and said, 'That's a great view, isn't it?'. We started chatting about the Castle and the Cathedral, and then carried on commenting on the various sights we saw as we travelled through the glorious English countryside. The young man next to Ben started to occasionally look up from his laptop to listen to what we were saying, and then he began to look at what we were pointing out to each other. As we approached his stop, he packed away his work, and as he stood to leave, he said 'Thank you. I've done this journey a hundred times and have never bothered to look out of the window. Now I know what I have been missing.'

But sometimes we miss out on something not because we are distracted, but because we are just too familiar with what we are seeing, or what we are saying, and that is sometimes the danger with our worship, and even with our reading of the Bible. At a funeral last year, the family chose Psalm 23, The Lord is my Shepherd. It is one of the most well-known passages in the Bible, and certainly the most well-known Psalm, but is it too familiar? In my talk, I focused on the line 'Yea, though I walk through the valley of the shadow of death', and especially on the word 'through', and pointed out the hope and promise that that line gives. We don't walk into the valley; we walk through it. After the service, one of the mourners said that she had always thought the psalm to be sad and depressing, but now she could see that it was full of hope and love; it had just become too familiar.

On a Sunday morning, it would be easy for me to get caught up in the familiarity of the service and to say the words by rote, out of habit, and not to focus on their meaning, their importance, and their awesomeness, and for the congregation to do the same. Indeed, a few years ago, a fellow Priest in a church in Chichester turned two pages of his service book at once and missed saying the Lord's Prayer. It was only as he started to say the final blessing did he realise what he had done!

I once said that the Sunday I no longer feel the hairs on the back of my neck stand up as I say the words 'Take, eat; this is my body which is given for you' will be the Sunday I know that it is time for me to stop, because I will no longer be offering myself totally and completely to God, will not be offering a sacrifice of praise and thanksgiving, and will be failing in my service to Him, and to his people, because I will have become distracted, or will have let the words, and their awesome meaning, become over familiar.

So, when you read your Bible, or when you sit in church and listen to the words of the readings, and the Eucharistic Prayer at the altar, don't let familiarity rob you of the joy, rob you of the promise they bring, or rob you of their awesomeness and wonder, because God sent his only begotten son, so that all who believe in Him may have ever lasting life.

15th July 2022

Every day, after breakfast, my sister feeds her sour dough starter. A spoonful of water and a spoonful of flour. In winter, the jar is then taken to the airing cupboard to allow the natural yeast to work. In summer, it sits happily on the kitchen worktop. Once a week, when there is enough starter, she makes a loaf. After mixing, kneading, and proving, the loaf is ready for the oven. The baking stone is heated to the required temperature, the dough is shaped, and we're off.

But it doesn't always turn out as expected or anticipated. This week's loaf was a little flat! Well, in fact, it was very flat. What went wrong? What should have been done differently? Well, nothing. The recipe was followed, and the oven temperature was right; it's just one of those things. (Well, to be honest, we did blame the weather, but then at the moment we are blaming the weather for everything!). However, although the loaf may not be perfect to look at, it is fit for purpose. It still tastes delicious; it still makes amazing sandwiches and great toast for breakfast.

But we all like to strive for perfection, don't we? I'm sure all the people making cakes and biscuits for the Singleton Fete tomorrow are far to experienced, and talented, to have to have several attempts at baking, as I would have to, but even if what they generously produce is not perfect, they will still be fit for purpose, and more than that they will still be delicious, they will still make our mouths water when we see them, and they will still make us happy when we eat them.

One of the biggest issues in the world today, especially for children and young people, is the apparent need to strive for perfection. The need to live up to what they, we, see on social media and on TV. Images of perfect happy families. Images of beautifully made-up women and well-groomed men. But how much of it is real? It is estimated that someone will take up to 25 selfies before they get the perfect shot to post on Facebook. People post about the great things that are happening in their lives, but rarely about the not so great. For every post that shows a wonderful life, there are numerous events in all our lives that are never posted, because they show the sad times, or the less successful times. The post that says someone has just got the perfect job is rarely preceded by posts of how many other job applications went in without even getting an interview.

One of the most confusing quotes from the bible, from Jesus, is from The Sermon on the Mount. After telling his disciples, and us, how we should live, Jesus says we should 'Be perfect, therefore, as your heavenly Father is perfect.'. But how can we be perfect? We're human with all our faults and failings; we can never be as perfect as God, and striving for that perfection leads to unhealthy comparisons, and unhealthy competition. But Jesus is not telling us that we need to be perfect as we see perfection; what he is telling us, asking us, is that we strive to be the best us we can be. Just as with my sister's loaf of bread, Jesus wants us to be fit for purpose. He wants us to make the best of who we are. Yes, we will fail sometimes, but Jesus knows that, God knows that, and accepts it, because we are human, and because He loves us.

Jesus accepted the imperfections in those he called to serve him, and he accepts our imperfections. After all, Peter, the Rock on whom Jesus chose to build his church, denied him 3 times. Hardly the behaviour of a perfect disciple, but Jesus loved him and forgave him. Thomas doubted Christ's Resurrection, but Jesus loved him and forgave him.

If Jesus loved and forgave those who had travelled with him, those who had seen first-hand the miracles, the healings, the casting out of demons, how much more will he forgive us. If Jesus didn't demand perfection from them, in their lives, in their service, how much more will he not demand perfection from us?

116

Jesus calls us to be the best we can be, knowing who we are, and what we have to give. He calls us not to strive for a perfection we can never attain, but for a completeness of who we are. If we pray not to have the life others appear to have, but to be not only content with our own lives, but to live that life in all its fullness, then we will have answered Jesus' call to be perfect as God is perfect. God is perfect, complete, fit for purpose, as who He is, and that is all He asks of us, to be what he calls us to be, the best 'us' we can be, in the service of God and in the service of others.

29th July 2022

It's funny how sometimes things we take for granted can cause confusion, isn't it? Outside St Olav's Bookshop, we have 2 information boards. One lists the opening times of the shop and the other gives details of the church. They have been there, in one form or another, for as long as I can remember, and I suppose because I have always known it to be both a shop and a church, they make perfect sense to me. However, we get quite a few visitors who come in and ask where the church is, and can they get to see it. After explaining that they are, in fact, in the church, I launch enthusiastically into a brief history of the building, and sometimes a brief history of Chichester. Whilst most are grateful that, by using it to house a bookshop, the building is still standing and still a place of worship and of faith, a few express disappointment that they can no longer see it with pews, altar, and font. That we have, as one gentleman put it, 'gone over to the other side'!

The thing about St Olav's is that it only exists as a bookshop because it is housed in a consecrated church, and it has only been able to survive as a consecrated church because it houses a Christian bookshop. The one is supported, enabled, and made possible by the other. The same applies to me. I can only serve as Priest and Rector of the Valley Parish because of my work in the bookshop, and I can only provide the often-needed pastoral support to customers and visitors because of my calling as Priest, supported and enabled by the people of the Parish.

One half of my life is not possible without the other, just as neither St Olav's Christian Bookshop nor St Olav's Church would exist without the other. And the same applies to the life of the church and the parish here, in the valley. The Rector, Churchwardens, PCC, congregations, and indeed our buildings, cannot exist in isolation. We rely on each other, and the wider community to enable worship and to offer support and help in whatever way we can.

But at the heart of what we do, here in the Valley and in St Olav's, must be the love of God. It is the foundation, the rock, the constant, at all times and in all situations, but most importantly, it is a love that is offered freely and equally to all, irrespective of age, race, gender, ethnicity, to those of faith and to those of none. It is a love that is there when we pray, it is there when we doubt. It is there when we are at work, it is there when we are at play, when we are busy, and when we are still. It is a love that God wants us to share in and to share with others.

119

As St Paul's wrote, 'Love is patient; love is kind; love is not envious or boastful or arrogant or rude. It does not insist on its own way; it is not irritable or resentful; it does not rejoice in wrongdoing, but rejoices in the truth. It bears all things, believes all things, hopes all things, endures all things. Love never ends.' (1 Corinthians 13: 4 – 8a). If we have that at the heart of all we do, and all we say, and all we are, then we can, and will, make the world a better place, starting today.

5th August 2022

We've had a lot of visitors at the Rectory this week, and they've all arrived for breakfast! The usual sparrows, starlings, pigeons, and goldfinches have been joined by thrushes, the partridges are back, and a woodpecker has discovered the joy and the ease of the birdfeeder!

What I love about watching the birds is not just the variety we get to see, but the way they all accept each other and how they all share the space on the feeders, waiting, albeit maybe a little impatiently, for a perch to become free. The smaller birds, although probably unintentionally, dislodge seeds that provide rich pickings for the pigeons and partridges, and the starlings, moving across the lawn in great numbers, are hopefully picking up all the seeds from the weeds, preventing their spread, and saving us humans some work in the bargain.

But all is not perfect in the bird world. We noticed yesterday that one of the starlings has a withered foot, which can take no weight. But it didn't stop him, or her. They happily hopped across the lawn on one foot, clung to the side of the feeder with one claw, and of course, could take to flight at a moment's notice.

They were also not excluded from the flock or treated differently.

Inclusivity and accepting everyone as equal and valued is in the news a lot at the moment, especially within the Christian press, and we can learn a lot from the birds in the garden, and from the Commonwealth Games currently taking place in Birmingham.

Unlike the Olympics, there are no performance criteria set before the event to qualify, and so athletes, swimmers, gymnasts who would never make it on to the Olympic stage are able to compete for their homeland, be it Australia or Jersey, Canada or Sri Lanka, giving their best, whatever their ability, or disability, sharing in their love of the sport. For the first time, the Para Games are running not just concurrent with the main event, but fully integrated into it. There is one timetable of events and one medal table. The crowds in the various stadiums give their support to the first, and the last, in each and every event, often offering greater applause to the men and women who determinedly finish the race with no hope of winning, but unwavering in their desire to do their best, and give their best, for their country, for their teammates, and for themselves.

I have written often about God's call on us to be the best 'us' we can be, and also about the golden rule of the Christian faith, Treat others as you would wish to be treated, and that is what we see at the Commonwealth Games. Yes, the crowds have come to see the star performers, be it Katrina Johnson Thompson in the athletics, or Laura Kenny in the cycling, or Joe Fraser in the gymnastics, but they cheer on everyone because if they were out there, if they were competing, they would want to know that they were being supported, and valued, without judgement, without prejudice.

I don't know if the birds in the garden think about their friend with the withered foot as being different from them, or whether the starlings look at the sparrows and know that they are a different breed, but they coexist happily with each other, accepting their differences, and sharing in all that God has given in creation. The athletes who win the gold medals may be the best on the day, but they are also often the first to greet the swimmer, or runner, who came in last, because they know what they have given of themselves, they appreciate the effort they have made to be the best they can be, and that is to be celebrated and applauded.

Wouldn't it be a wonderful world if we all did the same, accepting of our different gifts and skills, celebrating the gifts and skills of others, and sharing in all that we have, loving each other as God loves us, equally and completely.

12th August 2022

I sat down at my desk this morning, turned on the computer, and with fingers poised over the keyboard, started to think about my Ramble today. The problem was, nothing came. My mind went blank, and I had what can only be described as writer's block. What to talk about? There is so much going on at the moment, there is so much I could reflect on, that I was a bit overwhelmed.

Should I talk about the hot weather? Well, by the time you read this, we may well officially be in a drought, and we all know the advice about keeping safe, about keeping cool. How about the rising cost of living? But do you really want to know about our situation at the Rectory? Then there is the continuing conflict in Ukraine. But what can I add that hasn't already been said in the news, on the internet, and on social media? None of that will stop me reflecting on these things in the future, but not today, today I had nothing to offer.

So, I did what I usually do at times of difficulty or confusion, I opened my Bible, randomly, and my eyes landed on the passage below.

'Do not worry about tomorrow, for tomorrow will bring worries of its own. Today's trouble is enough for today.' (Matthew 6: 34).

Well, that was certainly true of me, as I sat looking out over the Trundle, troubled by what to write, wondering about all the emails and phone calls I had to make, and letting them get in the way of clear thinking, and of doing what I have to do today.

Tomorrow will bring worries, issues, concerns, for many of us, and today isn't going to be easy for a lot of people, but is Jesus telling us that we should not think about tomorrow, and live for today? No, because we do need to plan, we need to prepare. Those in work need to plan for retirement. Farmers need to plan for future planting, and decide what will work in the changing climate. Parents need to plan for the rest of the school holidays. The PCC needs to plan for fundraising, and I and the Churchwardens need to plan for this Sunday and next, so how can Jesus tell us not to think about tomorrow?

 Well, He isn't. Jesus isn't telling us not to plan, not to be prepared, not to think about tomorrow; He is telling us not to worry about it. Before telling his disciples, and us, not to worry, He asked a question, 'can any of you by worrying add a single hour to your span of life?' (Matthew 6: 27).

I admit I am a bit of a worrier; I don't take to heart Jesus' words. I worry about next week, about next month, about next year, but does it help? No, it leads to sleepless nights and stressed days, not only not adding a single hour to my life, but wasting some of those I have. What I, what we, need to do is plan, be prepared, and to quote my old boss, 'control the controllable', and then to focus on what we can do today, and not what we can't.

So, after I have finished my Ramble and sent it out to you all, I will turn to the next task, and then the next. I will send out the readings for Sunday, and agree on the music. I will answer emails and make phone calls. I will do what I can today, and what I can't will be left for tomorrow, without worrying about what I couldn't do, but giving thanks for what I could.

19th August 2022

One of the things I love most about working in the bookshop is the variety of people we get through the door, the reason for their visit, and the questions that they ask.

Some come to look at the building, yes, we are still a consecrated church, but no, we don't have any photographs of what it looked like when it was first built in the 11th century.

Some come to buy a particular book, yes, we do sell lots of different bibles, but no, we don't have a first edition.

Some come to buy supplies for their church, yes, we do sell communion wafers, but no, they are not pre consecrated.

Whatever the reason for someone pushing open the door, conversations usually turn to faith, God, or the Church.

This week, I had a very interesting, and challenging, chat with a young woman from Yorkshire, whom I will call Jane. Jane was visiting family in the area and took the opportunity to buy a book that had been recommended to her by her local vicar. After discussing the Archbishop of Canterbury, the Lambeth Conference, and the state of the Church of England today, she turned to me and said 'Do you fear God?'. Before I could respond, another customer quoted from the book of

Proverbs (9:10) 'The fear of the Lord is the beginning of wisdom'. She then smiled at us both and left.

After a short pregnant pause, Jane said 'But I don't want to fear God. I know I should, we will all be judged, but do need I fear Him?' I didn't answer straight away, but asked her what had prompted her question. It turns out her local Vicar had done a series of sermons on judgement, on damnation, and on fearing God. Now I said last Sunday that I can't preach fire and brimstone sermons, but my colleague in Yorkshire obviously had no problem in doing so, and it had caused Jane to have sleepless nights, and to worry about everything she did and everything she said. To worry about whether she was good enough.

Now, I admit I am not able to quote chapter and verse from the Bible at the drop of a hat; my memory isn't wired that way, but some verses are ones that just stick, and the quote at the top of this Ramble is one of them, 'Fear not, for I have redeemed you. I have called you by name, you are mine' (Isaiah 43: 1). When challenged over the greatest commandment, Jesus didn't say to fear God, he said 'You shall love the Lord your God with all your heart, and with all your soul, and with all your mind." This is the greatest and first commandment.' (Matthew 22: 36-38).

So, I asked Jane if changing the word fear into respect in the quote from Proverbs would change the way she thought about God and about her life. If adding the word love would help her in her relationship with God, and with others. 'Love and respect of the Lord is the beginning of wisdom'. Again, there was a pregnant pause, and then she smiled and said, 'Yes, I want to please God because I love Him. I want to do what He asks because I respect and reverence Him.' Jane is going to come back to the shop the next time she is in Chichester, and I hope and pray that love will have replaced fear, and that hope will have replaced doubt.

'Fear not', or 'do not be afraid', occurs 366 times in the Bible. Love appears 551 times. The quote from Isaiah is the most frequently used in cards and on cakes to celebrate someone's ordination, the beginning of a life in the service of God and of his people, and it can be a scary prospect, but not one that is undertaken because of fear, but because of love.

God loves us and asks that we love Him, because through the death and resurrection of His Son, He has redeemed us, called us by name, and we are His.

130

15th September 2022

Marking the death of Queen Elizabeth II

As word began to spread last Thursday, across this country and around the world, that all was not well with The Queen, and newsreaders and presenters appeared in black, and members of the Royal Family made their way to Scotland, two words began to appear with ominous regularity in emails and on Clergy Facebook groups, London Bridge. London Bridge was, as many of you will know, the code for the death of Her Majesty. As I watched the news, and kept a close eye on emails and Facebook, we got the message that we all dreaded, London Bridge has fallen.

Like the Royal Households, the Government, and the Armed Forces, the Church had in place plans for London Bridge. Books of condolence were to be available in every parish, with a portrait of the most photographed woman in the world to be placed in every church. Special orders of service were available within 2 hours of the official news of her death, and from mid-afternoon on Thursday, we had people in place to toll the church bells, to mark the passing of our longest serving Monarch, our rock, our constant.

And that is the word I have heard most often on the news and special programmes, from people waiting in the rain for Her Majesty's coffin to return to Buckingham Palace, from the people of Edinburgh as they took on, with amazing dignity and respect, the mantle of being the first people of our Nation to honour her, and from the people queuing for hours to pay their respects at her Lying in State. She was our constant. She was always there, in good times and in bad, at times of great rejoicing and at times of great sadness, but now we have to come to terms with the fact that that winning smile will be seen no more, that her dignified figure will no longer be seen leading our Nations Act of Remembrance at the Cenotaph.

Because for all the plans, for all the preparation, for all the emails with guidance for how we should react to London Bridge, nothing could prepare us for what we have seen, heard, and felt over the past week.

Because The Queen was more than just our Monarch, more than just our Head of State, she was the anchor to which we could all cling when things got rough, she was the voice of reason and of experience, behind closed doors, when Prime Ministers didn't know which way to turn, and she was the person we all wanted to see, on the balcony at Buckingham Palace or on our TV screens, when the country needed hope and reassurance.

Queen Elizabeth II made no secret of what, and who, was the bedrock of her 70 plus years of service, of duty, and of love and loyalty to her people. She may have been the constant, the anchor, that we looked to, but her anchor, her rock, her constant, was God and her faith.

Jesus told his disciples, after His Resurrection, 'And remember, I am with you always, to the end of the age.' (Matt 28: 20), and that was a promise that The Queen not only believed in but relied on. She knew that whatever she faced, whatever we faced, Jesus was, is, and always will be with us.

As we prepare to say a last goodbye to the Queen, to come together on Sunday as a community to offer our grateful thanks for her service and example, and on Monday as a country, a commonwealth, a world, to acknowledge the wonderful example she gave of service, of duty, and of love, I pray that we can all find comfort in knowing that Jesus will be with us, and her family, in our grief, and will give us, and them, the strength to follow her example, and to commit ourselves to the service of God and of each other.

Gracious God, we give thanks for the life of
your servant Queen Elizabeth,
for her faith and her dedication to duty.
Bless our nation as we mourn her death and may
her example continue to inspire us;
through Jesus Christ our Lord. Amen.

14th October 2022

I have been reflecting lately on generosity, on the giving of time and talents, on the sharing of resources. The miracle of the Feeding of the 5000 (John 6; 1 – 14) is one of the most well-known acts of Jesus' ministry, but how often do we remember that it began with a simple act of generosity? As the disciples are debating with Jesus, and amongst themselves, as to how they are going to feed the 5000 men, women, and children, who have followed Jesus up the mountain, a small boy steps forward and offers them the 5 Barley loaves and 2 fishes that he has in his basket. To put it into perspective, the food he carried was probably all his family would have had for the day, and yet he offered it to Jesus for the benefit of others.

I was once accused of being a heretic because I suggested that the miracle that day, beside the Sea of Galilee, wasn't that Jesus turned the meagre offerings of a small boy into enough food for everyone, but that I believe the true miracle was that the people saw the selfless generosity of a child and decided to follow suit. No one set out on a journey in those days with no provisions. There were no shops along the road, no service stations or pubs, and so you took with you a little food, and a little wine, whatever you had in your cupboard.

Now I am not alone in suggesting that what really happened that day was the biggest Bring and Share Supper ever, more learned and holy men and women than I have also put forward this alternative Miracle, including the former Archbishop of York, John Sentamu. And in suggesting that generosity was at its heart, we are not taking away any of the power of the miracle, nor questioning the people that day who declared Jesus to be 'The prophet who is come into the world'. Jesus' teaching, Jesus' compassion, prompted the child to step forward, and inspired those there, the poor, the meek, and the outcast, to share what they had, and that is a true miracle of love and service if ever there was one.

Over the past couple of weeks, at our Harvest Festival Service, the Harvest Lunch, and in our schools, so many of you have followed the example of the small boy in sharing what you have with those who have nothing, through Food Bank Collections and donations. I don't know exactly how much food has been given by the people of The Valley, but I know of at least 30 Bags for Life that were filled with tins and packets, washing up liquid, and shower gel. I know that the generous donation of over £200 at the Harvest Lunch will provide 28 people with a 3-day food parcel, plus practical support and advice.

Jesus' message of love, his command to treat others as you would wish to be treated (Matt 7: 12), is at the heart of the Miracle of the Feeding of the 5000 and is at the heart of what we do. It is what prompts men and women to offer their time and talents to the RNLI. It was what made so many offer help and support during the pandemic. In the musical Cabaret, we are told that 'money makes the world go round', but much of that money is raised by charities through their shops, which rely not just on the generosity of donors, but also on the time given by volunteers. Cathedrals and Abbeys may have staff to help run them, but local churches reply on the generosity of their people, both members of the regular congregation and the wider community, to provide not just the money for heating and lighting, but also the music, the flowers, the tea and coffee after the service, and the opening of the church doors on a daily basis for those who need a place to sit, in peace and quiet.

At the end of the passage in John's Gospel, we are told that the disciples gathered up 12 baskets of left-over bread. Am I wrong in believing that that surplus would have been given to the people as they left, to see them through their journey home, and to provide them with food for the next day?

We are all facing difficult times, with rising food prices and energy bills, but we are, with a roof over our heads and a meal on the table, richer than over 75% of the world's population. So, as we face what many are predicting will be another Winter of Discontent, remember the small boy with his loaves and fishes, and his generosity, remember that it is in giving that we receive, give thanks for all you have, and share your blessings, your gifts, your talents, and yes, maybe, even your time.

Lord, make me an instrument of Your peace;
Where there is hatred, let me sow love; Where there is injury, pardon;
Where there is discord, harmony; Where there is error, truth;
Where there is doubt, faith;
Where there is despair, hope; Where there is darkness, light;
And where there is sadness, joy.
O Divine Master, Grant that I may not so much seek
To be consoled as to console; To be understood as to understand; To be loved as to love.
For it is in giving that we receive;
It is in pardoning that we are pardoned;

And it is in dying that we are born to eternal life.

(Prayer of St Francis of Assisi)

21st October 2022

Our Mum was a great believer in not wasting food, in using left overs. Maybe it was because as a child, growing up in the country, money was tight, and a trip to the shops was a major expedition. Maybe it was a result of rationing during the war. Or maybe it was simply that she couldn't bear to see anything go to waste. Whatever the reason, very little food ever made it into the bin or even the compost heap. It is a philosophy and practice that my sister and I carry on, and I know so do many of you.

But there is a lot of food wasted in this country and around the world. In 2020, it was estimated that UK households threw away 4.5 million tonnes of food, much of it still in its packaging. On top of that, producers, supermarkets, and restaurants threw away a further 5 million tonnes of often perfectly edible, fresh food, mostly fruit and vegetables.

At the WI meeting this week, we heard about UK Harvest (www.ukharvest.org.uk), a charity set up with three aims. To rescue food, to redistribute that food, and to eliminate hunger through education, through the provision of cooking classes and easy to follow recipes. To date, UK Harvest has rescued and redistributed over 2000 tonnes of food, surplus supplies from supermarkets, restaurants, producers, and supplied that surplus to individuals, community centres, charities, and homeless shelters, amongst others.

UK Harvest is doing amazing work to reduce the amount of food we waste each year, and to teach people not only how to cook, but also how to use the left overs. If she were still with us, our Mum would not only be accessing their services, she would probably be a volunteer!

Now some of you may be seeing a bit of a theme with my Rambles, as last week I reflected on the Feeding of the 5000 and the fact that it may well have been simply a miraculous case of everyone being inspired and moved to share what they had, much as UK Harvest work to share the surplus food from big, and small, businesses. I also suggested that the left overs, all 12 baskets, wouldn't have gone to waste but would have been given to the crowd to take home, to use the next day, with a little meat, or fish, or oil, added for flavour and bulk.

But this week I have been thinking about what else we waste. What opportunities to share our blessings, to offer a kind word, to help someone in need, do we waste, not because we don't want to help but because we are either too busy, too distracted, or often unsure of what to do or what to say. A friend of mine, in a large urban parish that runs a food bank, a homeless shelter, and a community hub, is often thanked for the work he and his amazing team of volunteers do. His reply, always humble and always affirming, also always includes one simple but effective request, now go pay it forward. Each person who comes to them to receive a hot meal, or a bag of much needed groceries, or a bed for the night, is asked to take their blessing and pass it on, in whatever way they can. It might be simply by saying hello, with a smile, to the elderly lady they see every day at the bus stop. It might be in offering to collect a food parcel for their neighbour. But sometimes they are called to do more. Most of the volunteers at the homeless shelter were, or still are, homeless themselves, but they want to make sure others receive the warmth and support they themselves benefited from.

I have often spoken of the Golden Rule of Faith, Treat others as you would wish to be treated, and I make no apology for repeating it, as it should be at the heart of all we do. It isn't a uniquely Christian rule; indeed, it is believed to have its basis in Confucian times, 500 years before the birth of

Christ, and in 1993, over 140 leaders from the world's major faiths all endorsed it as a step towards a global unity and a global ethical view. But when added to Jesus' commandment to love our neighbour as ourselves, when that neighbour could be next door, in the next street, the next town, or halfway round the world, it is a powerful message, and a powerful appeal and command, to us all.

At this time, many people, in this country and around the world, are facing a difficult and challenging future. We can't, as much as we would like to, solve all the world's problems from our little corner of West Sussex, but we can make sure we don't waste any opportunity to share what we have, and who we are, and to pay it forward. A simple smile, a heartfelt thank you, a few tins in the foodbank collection, a donation to a refugee charity, or a few hours volunteering, all of these may seem small and insignificant in the scale of things, but if we all give a little of ourselves, and pay forward what we have received, we can be the instigators of something big, something meaningful, and something that may change someone's life for the better.

UK Harvest, Mary's Meals, and The Trussell Trust, all charities that have a huge impact on thousands of people's lives, were all started by groups of people with one aim, to

142

share their blessings and to make a difference. We may not be at the start of a major charitable enterprise, but as Jesus told us in Matthew's Gospel (13: 31-32), from the mustard seed, the smallest of all seeds, grows a great tree.

So, each day, let's all look at ways of paying forward the blessings we have received, the good news we have to share, and who knows where it may lead, who it may help, and how much of a difference we can make.

4th November 2022

Last week, I was on an Individual Guided Retreat. Each day, I met with my guide to talk about, well, whatever I wanted to talk about. There were 11 of us on the retreat, and each of us was there for a different reason. Some wanted to try and discover where God wanted them to go next, some wanted to have some time away from busy lives and busy parishes, and some, like me, wanted to simply spend more time with God, time that isn't always possible in the hurly burly of life.

At the first meeting, my guide asked me when, and how, I knew that God was calling me to the Priesthood, to the ordained life, and I could tell her exactly when. After years of saying no to the people who were encouraging me, after years of saying no to God, I went to a friend's Ordination

Service. It was a beautiful service, with wonderful music, and a great sermon, but of course, the big event, the reason we were all there, was to see the Bishop lay his hands on Peter's head and to make him a Priest. Just before Peter was called forward, we all stood to sing another hymn. The hymn was 'I, the Lord of Sea and Sky'. I had sung it a hundred times before, but as I sang the chorus, 'Here I am Lord, is it I, lord?' I knew, deep inside, that God was calling me. I knew that I couldn't keep saying no.

As I told my story, I was expecting my guide to suggest a bible passage for me to go and reflect on, to immerse myself in, but she didn't. She smiled, paused, and said 'Ok, so today go walk the grounds (the monastery I was staying in has 20 acres of open spaces and woodland) and reconnect with that moment. Sing the hymn, out loud or to yourself, and see where it takes you'.

So, I set off, in the rain, and began to sing. It was wonderful, and liberating, and awesome, but after a while the song morphed into another, and I found myself singing 'This is me' from The Greatest Showman – 'I am brave, I am bruised, I am who I'm meant to be, this is me'.

When I met with my guide the next day, I admitted, a little shamefaced, what had happened. Again, she smiled and

144

quoted from Isaiah 'I have called you by name, you are mine' (43:1).

God has called each of us, is calling each of us, and wants us to answer, 'Here I am, Lord,' but he also knows that we are broken, bruised, human beings, and that is what he loves about us. We are individuals, we are unique, and we come with all sorts of gifts and skills, but also with all sorts of doubts and fears.

In the modern world, there are so many pressures to be something, someone we're not. It could be pressure from family or friends, from our bosses, from our colleagues, but it isn't pressure from God. Yes, God wants us to grow in faith and love, to be the best us we can be. Yes, he wants us to get closer to him, to let him into our lives, through prayer and through worship, but he is calling each of us by name, who we are, where we are. He doesn't want us to be someone else; he wants us to be us.

As the week went on, my guide did give me bible passages to reflect on, but each of them reaffirmed that God wants us as we are, broken, bruised, imperfect. I reflected on St Peter, the rock on which Christ built his church, and all the apparent mistakes he made, and the times his faith seemed to fail him. I reflected on Jesus, in the Garden of

145

Gethsemane, asking God to take away the cup that would lead to his crucifixion, and on the cross, asking why God had forsaken him. If Jesus, the Son of God, fully divine as well as fully human, could question, could doubt, then how much more will God forgive us our times of doubt, our times of apparent failure to be the person he wants us to be, the person he has called us to be, the best us we can be.

So today, and every day, remember that God has called you by name, that you are his, broken, bruised, but loved, and pray that with his help, his grace, you will be the best you, the one you are meant to be, and that you can say or sing, with a loud voice, 'Here I am, Lord.' confident in his love, confident in his call.

11th November 2022

Who is my neighbour?

Do you remember the events of Wootton Bassett, or Royal Wootton Bassett as it is now?

From 2007, servicemen and women who had been killed in Iraq or Afghanistan were repatriated to RAF Lyneham. The base was only 5 miles away from the town of Wootton Bassett, and so the coffins, covered in the Union Flag, were driven through the town on their way to the John Radcliffe Hospital in Oxford.

As the first couple of hearses made their way through, a few people stopped at the side of the road and bowed their heads in respect. When the next ones came through, more people stopped. Then shops began to shut, and staff and customers would come and stand in respectful silence. As time went on, the local schools would make their way to the centre of the town, to join with former soldiers, in honouring those who had died.

By the time the base at RAF Lyneham closed in 2011, the streets of Wootton Bassett were lined with 1000's of people, from across the country, who had travelled to the small market town for one purpose, and one purpose only, to honour those who had lost their lives in the service of their country and to show their families and friends that they were not forgotten.

It is easy, on Armistice Day or Remembrance Sunday, to focus our attention on those who died in the two World Wars. Their names are on Memorials in our churches, the Poppy we wear in support of them grew in the battle-scarred fields of Flanders. But Remembrance isn't about a conflict a 100 years ago, or even just about those who died in foreign fields. Remembrance, respect, honour, is about asking ourselves the question Jesus was asked, Who is my neighbour?

The people of Wootton Bassett and those who travelled there, often from hundreds of miles away, didn't know the men and women who had died. They weren't from the local area; they had no connection with the town, other than that their final journey took them through the centre of a town with a big heart and a lot of compassion.

Jesus came to bring peace to a troubled world, but he charged his disciples, he charged us, with taking that peace out into the world, in spreading the Good News of the Kingdom of God, so that, as we read in the Book of Isaiah, 'They will beat their swords into ploughshares and their spears into

148

pruning hooks. Nation will not take up sword against nation, nor will they train for war anymore.' (Isa 2: 4)

Sadly, men, women, and children, military and civilian, are still dying on a daily basis because of wars, oppression, and persecution, and sometimes we feel helpless in not being able to do anything. Not being able to stop the fighting, the bombing, the pain. But as we gather to remember those who have died, those we knew personally and those whose names are in our churches, we need to remember that question, the question the lawyer asked Jesus, Who is my neighbour? Jesus' response was to tell the story of the Good Samaritan, the story of a stranger helping a man in need. We need to remember the people of Wootton Bassett, strangers who gathered to honour strangers.

If we can look at the world, not as a place full of strangers but as a place full of our neighbours, then we can, with faith, prayer, and perseverance, make a difference; we can beat swords into ploughshares, we can bring peace, we can bring hope.

2nd December 2022

Are you a Holmes or a Watson?

Don't worry, I'm not going to start a psychological analysis of Conan Doyle's famous creations, Sherlock Holmes and John Watson. No, I am talking about cats. To be precise, the two cats I had when I lived in my flat in Chichester. I got the brothers when they were 8 weeks old from a neighbour of my Mum. I really only wanted one kitten, but as they were going to be indoor cats, my Mum and Sister decided that one would get lonely with me at work all day, and so arrived with two. They were right, of course, and the three of us lived happily together for 18 years, before first Holmes and then Watson sadly died.

Like most human siblings I know, the brothers had very different personalities, whilst still being devoted brothers. They would have the odd fight, and then settle down together for a sleep, often so entwined that it was hard to see where one started and the other ended. In fact, the only way to tell them apart, both being jet black, was by a small white spot under Holmes' chin, and of course by their characters.

The difference in their personalities really showed when they were hunting. Now, as I said, they were indoor cats, and so their only prey was flies and spiders, the latter being one I was particularly grateful to them for. When hunting or chasing flies, Holmes would run around frantically, following the fly over chairs, sofas, across window sills, and leaving havoc in his wake as he knocked lamps and ornaments off of the sideboard. He rarely caught one. Watson, on the other hand, would sit patiently, calming, on the arm of a chair or the window sill, and watch the fly as it made its way around the room. Inevitably, it would, at some point, come within range, and then he would very effectively swipe it with his paw. The same difference showed in catching spiders. Holmes would be under the sofa, or trying to jump up the wall, while Watson would sit on the floor and wait.

Now you may be wondering where I am going with this. What has the personality of cats got to do with Advent, Christmas, or Christ?

Well, as we are now well into Advent, and Christmas preparations have started in earnest for many with the opening of the first Advent Calendar window, it is easy to get pulled into being a Holmes. There is so much to do. Cards to be bought, written, and delivered. Presents found and wrapped. Friends and family to be visited, or at the very least phoned, social events to be planned, and drinks and dinner invitations to be answered, and events hopefully attended. There are meals to be planned and extra food and provisions to be bought. There are cakes and puddings to be made, although for traditionalists, puddings were made last week, on Stir Up Sunday. For the clergy, there are extra services to be organised, more sermons and homilies than usual to be written, and carols to be chosen, appropriate to the service and the congregation. Sometimes it can seem as if 'frantic' is an understatement.

But in all the busyness, in all the activity, we also need time to be Watson. Not calmly waiting to swipe a fly or catch a spider, but calmly, patiently, expectantly, waiting for the birth of Jesus, the coming of the Light of the World. It may be by spending time with a daily reflection, it may be by spending time in prayer, or it may be by spending time, as Watson did, just sitting, just being. Advent is a time of anticipation, of expectation, and we can only truly embrace that anticipation if we take time to think about, to reflect on, what we are waiting for.

Last week, we lit the first Advent Candle in church, the candle that represented the Patriarchs, the founding Fathers of the Jewish Faith, such as Abraham, Isaac, and Jacob. They were men of faith, yes, but they were also men of action.

They could be compared to Holmes, examples of 'doing' in faith. This week, we light the candle for the Prophets, those who proclaimed, thousands of years before it happened, the coming of the Messiah, the coming of the Son of God, and the Son of Man. People such as Moses, Elijah, Isaiah, and Deborah. The Prophets knew about patiently waiting, knew about 'being' in the presence of God. They were also people of action, but the 'being', praying, giving time to God, was more important, and was the bedrock of all they did. They were the Watsons.

As we journey through Advent, I pray that I, and you, will find the time, and the commitment, to 'be' as well as to 'do'. That we will be able to channel our inner Watson as much as we channel our inner Holmes.

16th December 2022

Here we go a wassailing!

This week has been wonderful for me, because I love Christmas Carols and I have sung, over 3 days, almost all of my favourites.

On Monday, I had the privilege of joining staff and volunteers at the Weald and Downland Living Museum for their Carol Evening, and on Wednesday, the children and staff of West Dean Primary School welcomed family and friends to their Carol Service in St Andrew's. Both evenings were brilliant, and I have to say a special thank you and congratulations to Year 6 for their readings and prayers, and Reception for their wonderful Nativity Tableau.

But the highlight of the week, and I hope the Museum and School will forgive me, was Tuesday, when over 60 adults and children braved the cold to bring a little bit of Christmas cheer to Singleton, wonderfully led by the Singleton School Choir. I don't know about you, but I think there is something very special about singing carols outside, when it is cold and dark, our way lit by torches and lanterns. Of course, the Mulled Wine and Mince Pies we enjoyed helped, but it was an amazing evening and really put me in the Christmas Spirit.

But there is more to Carol Singing than simply coming together, around a fire, in a church, or walking through the streets.

Saint Augustine said, "Anyone who sings, prays twice", and through singing our favourite songs and carols, we learn and remember the wonderful, amazing story of Christ's birth, and the story of faith, and we get to tell it, to share it, through those songs and carols.

From our carols, we learn that Jesus shares our sadness as well as our gladness; he weeps with those who weep and rejoices with those who rejoice. We learn that when we hold those in need before God, we also know that our prayers are heard, because Jesus is already walking alongside them.

We learn that when we sing "Be near me Lord Jesus," we have already said a prayer, from out of our own needs, and we know that we are not alone.

We learn that the hopes and fears of all the years are met in the Christ child, on Christmas night and every night.

And, thanks to a new Carol I have learnt from West Dean School, we learn that on that first Christmas Day, love shone down, over the hills and over the valleys, and it still shines down, every day, over the whole world.

And we learn that the first Carol, the first Song of Christmas, was sung to the Shepherds as they watched their flocks by night. 'All Glory be to God on hight, and on the earth be peace, goodwill henceforth from heav'n to all, begin and never cease.'

But carols also remind us that for all that God has given us, through His Son, he also asks something from us, 'What can I give him, poor as I am? If I were a shepherd, I would bring a lamb; if I were a wise man, I would do my part, yet what I can I give him; give my heart.

Isn't that a song worth singing, and a message worth telling?

31st December 2022

Do you make New Year's resolutions? I admit that I used to, but I don't anymore. My resolutions were the usual suspects, eat more healthily, lose weight, take more exercise, and I did start off with the best of intentions, but it didn't take long for me to fall off the wagon, so to speak. The left overs from Christmas still needed using up, so the losing weight didn't happen, friends and family celebrate birthdays in January, so the healthy eating went out the window, and a cold, wet day gave me the perfect excuse to take off the walking boots, put on the slippers, and settle down on the sofa.

For me, breaking a New Year's resolution carried with it more guilt, disappointment, and a sense of finality than breaking the same resolutions at any other time of the year. Deciding to try and lose a bit of weight in May, ready for a holiday or a family celebration, didn't end because of one night out. I would just accept that the diet was on hold and begin again the next day, or maybe the next week. But break a New Year's resolution and I would throw in the towel immediately, and then spend a few days berating myself for my lack of will power. I don't know why, and I don't know if it is just me who feels that way. Maybe it is because after the joy and celebration of Christmas, a major change of routine, often involving some sort of restriction, was hard. Maybe it was because January is so often a dark, wet, and slightly depressing month that I wanted that glass of wine or bar of chocolate to cheer myself up a bit. Whatever the reason, New Year's resolutions just didn't work for me.

For many Christians, and indeed for many clergy, the New Year's resolution that is often made is to pray more and to give more time to God, and in my experience, breaking that one carries with it an even greater feeling of guilt and of letting ourselves, and God, down than any other. But it shouldn't. God is far more understanding, forgiving, and loving of us than we are of ourselves. Over the Christmas period, and for clergy and congregations that begin weeks before the Big Day at the start of Advent, regular prayer life can be over taken by events. More services and events than usual have to be planned, school Nativities and Carol Services attended, and family and friends not seen for months are welcomed into our homes, or we into theirs. It is easy for the days to be so full, and so long, that setting aside time for God can be the activity that falls by the wayside and then, just as with the diet or the exercise program, we don't know how to pick it up again, so we commit ourselves to do more than we were doing before as a way of apologising to God, as a way of making amends.

But God doesn't want us to set ourselves up to fail. God doesn't want us to, for example, promise to set aside an hour a day in prayer, if our busy lives mean that most days we manage only 20 minutes, or less. God doesn't want us to make promises we, and He, know we cannot keep. As a Priest I am required to say Morning and Evening Prayer every day, but sometimes my Morning Prayer is said at lunchtime, and my Evening Prayer is said just before I go to bed, because events over which I have no control have turned my day upside down and something had to give, and that something was my time with God. It may seem a little odd that rather than let someone down, I would let God down, but it isn't. God, through His Son, told us to love one another, to treat others as we would wish to be treated, and to put others' needs before our own, and sometimes those needs are greater than my need to pray.

I do need my time with God, and God needs His time with me, but God isn't governed by the clock or by the calendar. God is always ready for us, always waiting for us, whenever we turn to him, whenever we stop for a few minutes, or for half an hour, or for an hour. When I was away a few months ago, we were told that, because we were on retreat, we didn't need to join the monastic community at Morning and Evening Prayer because our whole day was an opportunity to pray. We had no distractions, we had no mobile phones, no internet, nowhere we had to be, and so we could, and did, pray at times when in our normal lives it would have been impossible. I prayed in the mid-morning sun, sitting in the cemetery, I prayed walking round the grounds, and I prayed at quiet times in the church and in the chapels when the weather kept me indoors. I prayed as and when I could.

So, as we look forward to a new year, I pray that you will find time to be with God, that you will find time to stop for as long as you can and thank God for your blessings and tell God of your fears and doubts, of your pains and heartaches. I pray that you will find comfort and hope in knowing that He is always with you, that He asks nothing of you but to be the best you you can be, and to let Him walk with you every day.

May I wish you all a happy, blessed, and peace filled New Year.

13th January 2023

EVERY SAINT HAS A PAST
EVERY SINNER HAS A FUTURE

Don't tell the Book Club, but I often, well, almost always, flick to the last chapter of a book to check if it has the right ending. Do the right people fall in love, or does the right person get caught for a crime? I also sometimes, and don't tell my sister, will check out the last episode of a TV drama before we watch it to again make sure that it has the right ending, and especially to make sure that it doesn't have those annoying words 'to be continued' flashed up on the screen as the last scene fades!

My desire to know how a story ends in books and TV dramas makes it all the more interesting that I love the parables in the Bible, because they almost always leave me with the question, 'What happens next?'

This week, I officiated at a funeral in my training parish, and the family had chosen, as their reading, the Parable of Good Samaritan. As I reflected on the reading before the service, I began to ponder on 'what happened next' to the characters we hear about in what is probably the most well-known parable, and most often quoted. The story is topped and tailed by an exchange between Jesus and a lawyer, an expert in the laws and rules of the Jewish faith. The lawyer asks Jesus 'Who is my neighbour' and after telling the story of the Good Samaritan, Jesus answers, basically, 'everyone'. But what about the people we hear about in the story? Yes, I know, it is a made-up story to offer the lawyer, and us, guidance as to how we should live our lives, but it still intrigues me as to what might have happened next, if Jesus had continued the narrative.

I am totally confident that the Samaritan would return to the Inn on his way home, that he would pay the Innkeeper all he owed. I am also confident that the Innkeeper would do what was asked, that he would look after the bruised and battered man, tending his wounds and ensuring he was fed and watered. And I am sure that the man would recover and return to his day-to-day life. But what about the others? What about the robbers, the priest, the Levite?

Maybe I am too optimistic, maybe I try to see the good, the positive, in everyone, even if it is buried deep, but I wonder, indeed hope, could the priest and the Levite have had a

162

change of heart? I wonder if they might have walked a little further down the road, reflected on what they had seen, and turned back. Maybe the priest could have met the Levite, talked to him about the man they had both left beside the road, and walked back together? Maybe they might have bumped into the Samaritan, or seen him put the man on his donkey and followed him, and then offered to pay some of the costs of the care package he had set up? I don't know, and we'll never know what Jesus would have said if he had been asked how the story ended, but it is a wonderful hope and prayer to have, isn't it? The disinterested become interested, the too busy' stop and give time to the less fortunate, the 'too important' put their own status aside to help the poor and lowly.

And what about the robbers? I have travelled the road the Parable follows, from Jerusalem to Jericho, and although I was in a coach and not on foot, it is a barren, bleak road, and easy to imagine the time of Jesus with robbers and thieves around every corner. In my 'what next' scenario, did the robbers wait, out of sight, to see who came along the road after the helpless man? Did they talk amongst themselves as to whether the Samaritan was to be their next victim? Or did one or two of them see the selfless actions of a stranger and stop in their tracks? Could the Parable of the Good

Samaritan, if continued, have seen a change of heart amongst the thieves? Again, I don't know, and maybe that is a hope and a prayer too far, but it does happen. The direction of some people's lives is changed by the actions of another, even seen from a distance.

I have reflected on the picture at the top of this Ramble before, the quote from Oscar Wilde that hangs in the Rectory just inside the front door, but as I thought about the Parable of the Good Samaritan and especially about my vision, for want of a better word, of what might have happened next, the quote seems to sum up that vision. The Good Samaritan was a saint to the injured man, but he was, is, also human like us, and his life would not have been perfect all the time; he would have sinned in some way or other in the past, but it is for the wonderful act of love and compassion that we know of him. The priest, the Levite, and the thieves have sinned in the Parable, by attacking the man or by leaving him beside the roadway, but in my vision, they turn their backs on that sin and look to a better future.

None of us are perfect all the time, none of us can be called saints all the time, and even the greatest Saints of the church had faults, but we can all try. We can all commit to loving our neighbour, everyone, as we love ourselves, we can all commit to treating others as we would wish to be treated, and we can all do so confident in the unfailing love of God, and of His never-ending forgiveness when we fail or make mistakes.

Every saint does have a past, but the most important, the most awesome, the most wonderful thing to remember is that God's promise to me, to you, to everyone, is that every sinner has a future, with and in God's love.

24th February 2023 – The first Friday of

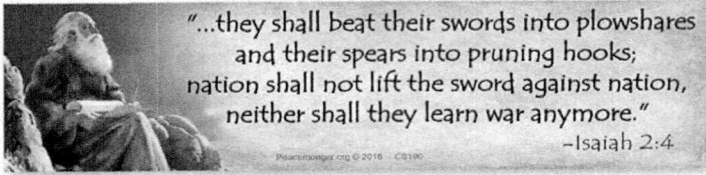

"...they shall beat their swords into plowshares and their spears into pruning hooks; nation shall not lift the sword against nation, neither shall they learn war anymore."

–Isaiah 2:4

Lent

I have struggled this week with what my Ramble, what my reflection, would be on. Should it be on Shrove Tuesday and Ash Wednesday, and the beginning of our season of Lent? Should it be on the effects of climate change and the impact on our food supplies? Should it be on the continuing war in Ukraine, as today marks the first anniversary of the Russian invasion? Or should it be on the growing divisions within the Church of England, and the wider Anglican Communion?

But as I was thinking about everything that is going on, my daily reading offered me the quote at the top of the Ramble. Now it could be said that it was a prophetic reading, given the situation in Ukraine, but it made me think, what would the world be like if we did all beat our swords, our tanks, into ploughshares? What would the world be like if instead of focusing on what divides us, on what we disagree about, we instead focused on what unites us, on our common ground, and worked for the common good? What would the world be like if the 2.5 billion Christians around the world stood up and said, enough is enough. What would the world be like if we joined with the other Abrahamic Faiths, the 1.7 billion Muslims, and the 15 million Jews, and said no, we're not going to fight, no, we're not going to decimate the worlds resources, no, we're not going to strip Africa and South America of its minerals and its food supplies just to make more and more goods for the west?

At West Dean School this morning, I had the privilege of making the sign of the cross in ash on those pupils and staff who chose to come forward. It may have been a couple of days late, but the meaning was the same, the emotion was the same, and the reverence and solemnity with which the children came forward matched that of those who came to our Ash Wednesday service, and it was truly humbling. When I made the mark of the cross, I said these words, 'Remember that you belong to God, and that God loves you'. What would the world be like if we all looked at each other with new eyes and remembered that we all belong to God? Not as his possession but in the same way we belong to our families, to our communities, to our schools. In the same way, we belong to the entire human race - part of one great big family,

There is, sadly, very little chance that the Christians, the Muslims, and the Jews, in Russia and Ukraine, will throw down their arms and say enough is enough, but what a wonderful world it would be if they did. There is very little chance that the different sides within the Church of England and the Anglican Communion will put aside their differences, but what a wonderful world it would be if they did.

Remember that you belong to God, and that God loves you. Remember that every man, woman, and child belongs to God, and that God loves every single one of them.

10th March 2023

There are some dates that not only go down in history, but where they were and what they were doing is engrained in the memory of all those around at the time.

20th July 1969 – The first moon landing.

22nd November 1963 – The assassination of JFK.

30th July 1966 – England win the Jules Rimet Trophy, the Men's Football World Cup.

But there is another 22nd November that I can remember, and I can tell you exactly where I was and what I was doing, as with pretty much the last kick of the game, Johnny Wilkinson secured the Webb Ellis Cup, the Rugby Union World Cup, for England in 2003.

I've been thinking about sport, and about rugby in particular, as the Six Nations Championship returns this weekend, for the penultimate round of matches. Now I admit that I am an armchair big match rugby fan, and an armchair big match football fan, but I have been to a couple of Pompey matches, and I have been to the home of England Rugby.

A few years before the glorious day in 2003, a friend was given two tickets for a match at Twickenham, or HQ as it is known. It wasn't a big match against Australia or New

Zealand, or one of the Six Nations against Wales, Scotland, or Ireland, but a friendly against Samoa in November. The match was brilliant, but what really struck me was the crowd. The match was a friendly, and so were all the supporters. There was no segregation of fans, and when we took our seats, we found ourselves sitting next to two Scotsmen, who shared a nip of whisky with us 'to keep the chill out', and behind a group of Samoans in national dress who must have been freezing! There was good natured banter between a group of Frenchmen in berets with onions around their necks and a group of Englishmen wearing three-piece suits and bowler hats. At half time, most of the crowd streamed out to buy refreshments and to stretch their legs, and when they returned, our two new friends from Scotland had brought us back some coffee and a burger! It was a wonderful example of the coming together of people with a common purpose, to enjoy a game of rugby, and a common goal, to make sure everyone else enjoyed it too!

The good nature of the crowd continued as we made our way back to the tube station after the match, swept along amidst a lot of singing and a lot of banter. In the streets around Twickenham, some of the locals had set up coffee stations in their gardens and even a couple of burger stands. The mounted policemen had nothing to do but accept the greetings from the fans, many of whom seemed to know them by name, and to stop their horses from being over fed by those who had come prepared with horse friendly snacks.

That game, on a freezing cold day in November, was the coming together of people of all ages, genders, races, and many nationalities. All were there as equals. It showed the best of humankind. Everyone there came together over what united them, and put to one side what divided them.

Wouldn't it be great if the whole world thought and acted as the thousands of people at Twickenham had that day? Wouldn't it be great if all people of faith could think and act as the strangers in the stands had? There is so much that we all share, there is so much that we all agree on, but we let our differences dictate our actions and our words. We focus on age, race, gender, and even our differences in beliefs, and ignore our united call to be children of God, loved equally and completely.

If I get to watch the match tomorrow, I will remember my one and only visit to the home of England Rugby and pray that that sense of coming together, that sense of a united purpose, that feeling of a common purpose, will spread beyond the stands and out into the whole world.

171

17th March 2023

This week we made our regular trip over to the Garden Centre to pick up bird seed, they're a ravenous bunch up here! Usually, when we arrive, my sister makes a bee line for the plant section, especially the area for those plants that maybe need a little bit of TLC to survive, and stocks up for the next couple of months. But not this time. Having done a bit of a tidy up in what we call the garden room, linking the garage to the house, she had 'discovered' lots of seeds that she had accumulated over the last few years. Most were free gifts from magazines or from friends, and some were seeds that she had harvested last year from our own garden. Not all of them are suitable for our garden, and some of them are things that she would never grow anyway, but amongst them were all the seeds she needed for our vegetable beds, and a few flowers to plant out in the front of the house, and so this year there are to be no new 'ready grown' plants, everything will come from seed.

Now, as most of you know by now, I am not a natural gardener and my inclination is to go with the easiest option, so I would be the one buying all the ready grown, healthy plants that we need and that can go straight into the garden. However, even I have to admit that there is something very exciting and joyous in waiting for the first signs of life in the seed trays that are already beginning to appear on the window sills in the sitting room. Within the next couple of months, there will be no space left for the usual houseplants that sit there as more and more trays will appear, replaced by bigger and bigger pots as the seedlings grow, until finally I am handed a trowel and told, in the nicest and simplest way possible, where and what to plant.

In thinking about the difference between waiting for tiny seeds to grow, slowly and with a lot of TLC, and buying an already established tomato plant or tray of herbs, it got me thinking about faith and how that can grow from a tiny seed, over many years, or can seem to come as an already strong and confident knowledge of who we are and who God is.

The obvious analogy is between the Emmaus and Damascus Road experience of faith. I know people, and sometimes envy them, who have had a Damascus Road experience. It may have been at a Christian Mission event, or when visiting a church, or when listening to a friend or family member talking about God and faith. Suddenly, they know and feel God's presence and commit their lives to serve him. They are amazing and life changing experiences, but they are rare. For most of us, faith and a desire to know more is a slow process that grows and takes root over many years. The seed of that faith may have been sown while at school, or by attending Sunday School, or by the faith and lives of our parents. It can seem that it sits dormant for years, or be very slow to grow, but it is there, and with the love of those around us, and the lives of those around us, it slowly gets stronger and becomes more deeply rooted in our lives.

A friend, a monk in the Benedictine Order, told me about a nun he had met whilst visiting a convent in France. The woman, in her 40's when he met her, had entered the convent at the age of 18 with the sure and certain knowledge that that was what God wanted her to do, and where God wanted her to be. It seemed to me, when he was telling me about Sister Maria, that she had had a Damascus Road experience. She knew what God wanted from her. But then he continued, and I realised that like most of us, her journey to a deep-rooted faith had been slow and sometimes painful. Although she had entered fully into the life of the convent and her calling to be a nun, she admitted to my friend that for 18 years, she just hadn't gotten it. She attended the Daily Offices, the services in the chapel, five times a day. She knew the words off by heart, but when it came to the quiet time, the time of personal prayer and contemplation, she would look around enviously at the other Sisters and wonder what they had that

174

she didn't. She told my friend that for 18 years she counted the bricks in the wall opposite her seat while the others prayed. And then slowly, over time, she stopped counting and began to listen. She stopped 'saying' the words of the offices and began to listen to them. She stopped 'doing' her duties as a nun and began 'being' her duties. As her lived faith grew, she went, as she always did, to weekly confession and told the Priest of how her experience of the Living God had changed. His response, having walked with her for the previous 5 years, was both a prayer, a thanks giving, and also an instruction. His only words were, 'Thanks be to God.'

Faith, however it is planted, is a living thing. It needs nurturing, it needs feeding, and it needs to be cared for, not just by us but by those around us. Sometimes it seems to be dormant, as it was for Sister Maria for 18 years, but it is still there. Sometimes it may seem to have died, when our reading of the Bible doesn't inspire us, or our prayers seem to be hollow or to fall on deaf ears. But, just as with the tiny seeds on our window sill, with a little bit of time, a little bit of care, and a lot of love, it will once again spring back into a strong and healthy faith, if we let it, fed and watered by the ever loving, every forgiving, and ever present, God, Father, Son and Holy Spirit. Thanks be to God.

24th March 2023

As I sit at my desk this morning, I can see signs of new life springing up outside my window. The grass is growing, the daffodils are beginning to flower (maybe a little later than most, but my sister tells me it is all to do with the variety), and buds are appearing on the shrubs, and even on my vine. But what faces me in the garden is a hedge, and at the moment I can see through it because it hasn't yet started to put forth its new growth, but it is still a hedge and a pretty impenetrable one at that. Beyond the hedge is the Glebe Field and the children's play area, and beyond that is what we call heart attack hill, and beyond that is the Trundle, all of which I can see. But I know that beyond the Trundle is Chichester, and beyond Chichester is the sea. I can't see them, but I know they are there.

The same can be said about life and about faith. We can often see where we want to be, where we want to go, in our lives but between us and our goal is what can seem to be an impenetrable hedge, or a high wall, which stops us in our tracks for a while, until we find a way round it, or a gate opens up for us. Then we can continue on our life journey, heading on to the next thing we have set our eyes and our heart on. But sometimes we know where we want to be, but we can't see it, and we don't know how to get there, and in those times, we may have to rethink our route, or rethink our plans, or even rethink our destination.

The letter to the Hebrews tells us that 'faith is the substance of things hoped for, the evidence of things not seen' (11:1). Just as I know that Chichester is beyond the Trundle but I can't see it, I also know that God is with me every day, and is in everyone and everything I see and encounter, but I can't always see him or hear him. Sometimes our faith is challenged by life events, by the death of a loved one, or by the diagnosis of a serious illness. Sometimes we ask where God is in wars or natural disasters. The answer is that he is here, there, and everywhere. We may not be able to see him or hear him, but just as we know Chichester is over the hill, we also know that God is walking beside us every step of the way. We know that God is sitting with us as we mourn, is holding our hand in the doctor's surgery, is supporting and loving the people of Turkey and Syria, is standing with the men fighting in Ukraine, and is strengthening the families that wait at home for news.

If we want to see God, we only have to look out of the window and see the beauty of creation, or hold the hand of a new born baby, or look into the eyes of the next person we meet, or sit in quiet reflection and listen to the birds or the lambs. Then we will have the substance of things hoped for and the evidence of things not seen, and then we will be able to see God.

31st March 2023 – Palm Sunday

'Look, your king is coming to you,

humble, and mounted on a donkey' (Matt 21: 5)

This Sunday, we will be celebrating the start of Holy Week with Jesus' arrival in Jerusalem on Palm Sunday. Most preachers, and most commentaries, describe Jesus' 'triumphant' entry and then follow it with 'humbly riding on a donkey', but as you can see from the quote above, the prophet Zechariah foretold that the King, the Messiah, would BE humble. Riding into the great city of Jerusalem on a donkey may be the opposite of pretentious, but is that a mark of humility in itself?

The dictionary definition of Humble doesn't really help either. 'Not proud or haughty', yes, but it also says 'offering everything in a spirit of deference or submission'. Is that humble, or could it actually be a form of arrogance in itself? Is humility that is based on exaggerated deference really a form of conceit or pride? Think Uriah Heep in David Copperfield. His form of exaggerated humility, almost begging people to contradict him and assure him that he is important and valued, has made its way into everyday language, with people who have never read the novel or even know he is a literary character, recognising that there is sometimes something false, something fake, about an individual's speech or actions when they portray an inflated humility.

My favourite, my preferred, definition of humility comes from C S Lewis in his book Mere Christianity, 'True humility is not thinking less of yourself, it is thinking of yourself less'. Humility isn't putting the needs of others before your own because they are MORE important than you; it is putting them first because they are AS important as you. Humility is treating others as you would wish to be treated (Luke 6: 31), equal in the sight of God.

The Lying in State of Queen Elizabeth II showed us humility in people we may not have expected it from, based on their public persona. Heads of State and members of the Royal Family were fast tracked, overtaking the hundreds of thousands of people waiting patiently to pay their respects, and that was understandable, and that was right. But some celebrities did the same; some celebrities believed that their time was more important than anyone else's, and they should be treated differently. But not David Beckham. Now I should admit that I wasn't a huge fan up to that point, but I am now. David Beckham, OBE, joined the queue to pay his respects to his Queen at 2 am in the morning and queued for 12 hours.

He didn't ask for, or want, special treatment. It wasn't a Uriah Heep moment; he didn't parade his humility, he didn't wait expectantly for someone to come along and take him to the head of the queue. He didn't think he was more important than anyone else in the queue, but neither did he think he was less important than anyone else. He may have been queueing to pay his respects to the Queen, but in doing so, he also paid his respects to everyone else who was doing the same.

As we come together on Sunday and as we prepare to celebrate, with shouts of Alleluia, the Risen Christ on Easter Day, I hope and pray that true humility will spread around the world. That the people in power, the people who make the decisions that affect our lives and the lives of our neighbours in Ukraine, in Russia, and all over the world, will not think of themselves as less than anyone else, but will think less of their own ambitions, their own desires, their own power struggles. That they will treat others as they would wish to be treated, and in doing so, make the world a better place.

'True humility is not thinking less of yourself, it is thinking of yourself less'.

21st April 2023

Last week, my sister and I visited the National Memorial Arboretum in Staffordshire. There are over 420 memorials to both military units and civilian organisations, from the Ambulance Service to the Women's Institute. The statue that used to stand guard at the entrance to the Roussillon Barracks in Chichester is there, and on our visit, we met a lady whose husband had served in the RMP and been stationed there for many years. She was one of many on a personal journey of remembrance and reflection, and as we walked around, we heard parents and grandparents telling children about the people and the conflicts that were being remembered by the statues, the gardens, and the trees.

At the heart of the Arboretum is the Armed Forces Memorial, created to remember the men and women who have lost their lives since the end of the Second World War. They include those who have been killed whilst on duty, in military campaigns, or as a result of terrorist attacks. The names are recorded first by year, then by service, Royal Navy, Army, Royal Air Force, and then in date order.

As I looked at the list of names, the wonderful song 'When I needed a Neighbour' by Sydney Bertram Carter came into my head, and especially the final chorus, 'And the creed and the colour and the name won't matter. I'll be there.'

Because on the memorial, there are no ranks listed, no ages, and no indication as to gender, race, creed, or religion. The names are simply initial and surname, with an acknowledgment of medals awarded, with no clue as to whether the recipient was just out of school or a seasoned professional, and no indication as to whether they were a private or a colonel. On the Armed Forces memorial, all are equal, all are remembered, and all were there when they were needed.

But there was another memorial that I found to be just as poignant, and maybe even more important – the Shot at Dawn Memorial. This memorial remembers the 309 soldiers who were shot at dawn during the First World War because of alleged cowardice or desertion, who have now all been posthumously pardoned. The memorial is on the outer edge of the Arboretum, not because it is forgotten, but because it is the first to have the early morning sun, the first to see the new dawn.

On the Shot at Dawn memorial, age and rank are listed, and it is a pertinent reminder that whatever our age, race, gender, social status, or bank balance, we can all be affected by fear, by doubt, by simply not being able to cope. The men who were shot at dawn were faced with unimaginable horrors on a daily basis and felt they had nowhere to turn and no one to turn to. We are fortunate that mental health and our mental wellbeing is now something that we can talk about, if we choose to, and we hope and pray that if we do, we will not be judged as the men who were shot at dawn were. We hope and pray that there will be someone there for us to support us, help us, and importantly, understand us and what we are going through.

But whatever you are facing, whatever fears, doubts, pains, or insecurities, I pray that you will also know the love and grace of our Risen Lord, Jesus Christ, who was the first to say ''And the creed and the colour and the name won't matter. I'll be there.'

5th May 2023

The Coronation of King Charles III

I'm sure most of you will be watching the Coronation Service tomorrow or at least catching up with the highlights if, like many, you still have to work during the day. It will be, I hope, a truly inspiring and beautiful occasion. The music will be awesome, the pageantry spectacular, and the cathedral stunning. But for all the pomp and circumstance, the service tomorrow is a Christian service, a service of worship and a service of commitment. The tone, not only of the service but also of the King's life, will be set by the very first words we will hear him say tomorrow. After everyone has processed in, the King will be greeted by a Chapel Royal Chorister, representing all young people of the United Kingdom and the Commonwealth, with these words 'Your Majesty, as children of the Kingdom of God, we welcome you in the name of the King of Kings'.

The King's response will be simple and profound, 'In his name, and after his example, I come not to be served but to serve.'

It seems like only yesterday that we were gathering to celebrate the Platinum Jubilee of the Late Queen, and giving thanks for her life of service and dedication. That life was, and is, the inspiration for our new King. He has served the longest apprenticeship in history, all done in the public eye, with every word and every action open to comment and criticism. Yes, he has made mistakes, haven't we all, yes, he has spoken out of turn, but again haven't we all, but few of us have been subjected to the sort of media attention and intrusion that he has faced his entire life, and yet his first words at his Coronation will be to recommit himself not just to the service of the people but also in the service of God.

Much has been made in the past about his wish, expressed many years ago, to be the Defender of Faiths rather than the Defender of the Faith, but he is, as was his mother, a committed Christian, and the service tomorrow will reaffirm that commitment. It will also, however, acknowledge the diversity of our nation, and of the commonwealth, and after taking the oath to uphold the Church of England, its doctrines and its teachings, the King will also offer this prayer

God of compassion and mercy
whose Son was sent not to be served but to serve,
give grace that I may find in thy service perfect freedom
and in that freedom knowledge of thy truth.

Grant that I may be a blessing to all thy children,

of every faith and conviction,

that together we may discover the ways of gentleness

and be led into the paths of peace.

through Jesus Christ our Lord.

Amen.

There is so much that unites us, as a nation, as a commonwealth, and as a world, which in fact far outweighs that which divides us. We all share the responsibility of stewardship of this earth, we all hope and pray for the same things, food on the table, a roof over our heads, a long and healthy life, and peace. That is true if you live in a mansion or in a slum. It is true if you wear Prada or Primark, handmade shoes, or go barefoot. I pray that the service tomorrow, and all the events happening in the Valley, in the country, and around the world, will remind us of all we share, of all that unites us, and will strengthen us to work together for the common good. I pray that wherever we are, and whatever we are doing, this Coronation Weekend will increase our sense of community and strengthen our bonds of love and friendship with our neighbours, wherever they may be, and I join with His Majesty in asking God to 'Grant that I may be a blessing to all thy children, of every faith and

187

conviction, that together we may discover the ways of gentleness and be led into the paths of peace' Amen.

At services up and down the country on Sunday, congregations will be singing the National Anthem and raising a glass to the new King - I hope that in doing so they, and we, will recommit ourselves to the service of others, in the service of God, as he will tomorrow.

12th May 2023

What else could I Ramble on this week but the events of last weekend. There were some wonderfully amazing moments, from the Gold State Coach to the music in the Abbey, home to coronations for almost 1000 years, and of course the breath-taking display of military personal from around the Commonwealth, and their awesome precision and professionalism.

But the main event, the main focus of the day, was the Coronation of King Charles III. There were some wonderfully ancient titles of those taking part, Bluemantle Pursuivant, Maltravers Herald Extraordinary, and of course, Gold Stick in Waiting, a title held by The Princess Royal. There were also references to modern Britain, the Gospel Choir, the inclusion of the leaders from the many faith communities, and the central role played by women, Penny Mordant, President of the Privy Council, and Dame Sarah Mullally, the Bishop of London, to name but two.

The whole event was spectacular and impressive. Where else in the world would that number of foreign heads of state mix with pop stars, TV personalities, and the hundreds of ordinary people invited not because of who they are, but what they do, the people who serve others, the people who put others first, the charity workers, the volunteers, 'the great and the good'. As Giles Brandreth said, "It is in being good that they have become great."

But what I found most moving was in fact the one part of the whole day that we didn't see. It was the anointing, when screens were put in place, the finery removed, and in a simple white shirt (and trousers of course) King Charles III took his place on St Edwards Chair to be anointed in the service of God and of His people. It was an incredibly personal moment, and an incredibly humbling one for the King and for us. At that moment, he and we were reminded that all are equal in the sight of God. After the anointing, still in a simple shirt, the King knelt at the Altar as the Archbishop of Canterbury prayed -

'Our Lord Jesus Christ.... pour down upon your head and heart the blessing of the Holy Spirit, and prosper the works of your hands: that by the assistance of his heavenly grace you may govern and preserve the peoples committed to your charge in wealth, peace, and godliness'.

That moment reminded me of my ordination, and the charge I and my fellow Ordinands received from the Bishop, 'In the name of our Lord, we bid you remember the greatness of the trust that is now to be committed to your charge. Remember always with thanksgiving that the treasure now to be entrusted to you is Christ's own flock, bought by the shedding of his blood on the cross.' It was and is a powerful and heavy calling, but the Bishop continued, 'You cannot bear the weight of this calling in your own strength, but only by the grace and power of God.'

But the grace and power of God is not limited to those called to be Monarch or Priest. The grace and power of God is a gift to us all, as is the care of his people. When I was ordained, I was surrounded by my own screen, not made of cloth but made of people, as fellow clergy came forward and also laid their hands on me, to offer their support and their love. Surrounded as I was, I was aware of only two things, the Bishop in front of me, and the power and love of God that surrounded me.

I pray that King Charles III, shielded at that moment from the public gaze he has been under his whole life, also felt that love and power as he was anointed and then knelt at the Altar before his God and our God. I also pray that you feel that love and power as you also answer the loving and powerful call to be God's children, to serve Him in serving others, and that the grace of God, and the power of the Holy Spirit, will inspire and enable you to fulfil that calling.

191

19th May 2023

Sitting down to write the Ramble today, I thought it would be easy, so much going on, so much to think about and reflect on, but as I put fingers to keyboard, I got what could only be described as writer's block. I ran a couple of ideas past my sister, who said, as only sisters can, 'boring!' And 'what are you trying to say?' Don't you just love sisters! But she had a point, my first thoughts were boring, and my second idea didn't have anything to say, and then it struck me, what do you say when you don't know what to say? Now, Mary Poppins had the right idea with 'Supercalifragilisticexpialidocious', but that doesn't work for most of us, most of the time, although it has stood me in good stead with a class full of 4-year-olds!

But what do you say when you are met with a situation you weren't expecting? When you hear about the death of a friend's husband or wife, when you are told a friend has been diagnosed with Cancer, or that a child or grandchild is in hospital. A recent post on a Clergy Facebook group asked for advice on what to say in a note to someone they didn't know, following the death of their mother, who had been a regular and committed member of the congregation. The priest had written some lovely words about the lady, but didn't know how to end because they felt that 'you are in my thoughts and prayers' was a little bland and meaningless. I, and a huge number of my colleagues, disagreed. In our post-modern world, full of scepticism, self-reliance, and, yes, the quick post on Facebook or WhatsApp before we move on, what can be more powerful, more comforting, and more intimate than to be told that someone is thinking of you, and praying for you? To know that someone, somewhere, has put aside their own worries or concerns, has put aside their own needs and wants, to stop and think about you, to stop and pray for you.

Every few months, I spend a day in the Cathedral in Chichester as a Day Chaplain. My duties are, on the surface, quite simple. Every hour, I mount the steps to the pulpit and lead whoever is there in saying the Prayer of St Richard and the Lord's Prayer. Before I begin, I invite all those in the Cathedral, visitors, volunteers, and staff, to stop wherever they are, whatever they are doing, and just to take a few moments to listen to, or join in with, the prayers. Once the prayers are said, I return to my other duty, which is to walk round and round the Cathedral. Now, as most of you know, I can talk for Britain, and as I love Chichester and the Cathedral, I engage as many people as I can in conversation. 'Are you visiting the area' is a great way to start, and more often than not, I get to hear all about a person's holiday or day trip, about who they are with that day, and even offer suggestions as to where to go next (I should get commission from the Pallant House Gallery).

But the most significant and meaningful conversations are those that move past day-to-day activities and on to deeper and more personal matters. It is a real honour and privilege to be there for people who want to talk about the recent death of a loved one, or the cancer diagnosis they have just received, but don't know who to turn to, or don't want to 'burden' the people closest to them. At times like those, the simple question 'May I pray for you' often has a profound and sometimes overwhelming affect. To know that someone is focusing on you, that someone is there for you, is one of the greatest gifts we can give, and letting someone do the same for us is one of the greatest gifts we can receive. As St Francis of Assisi said 'It is in giving that we receive'.

So, the next time you are stuck for words, the next time you are faced with a situation you weren't prepared for, remember that the greatest gift you can give is your time and your attention. That telling someone you are thinking of them, and praying for them, and will continue to do so, is worth more than anything else in the world because you are putting someone else first, you are putting someone else's needs above your own. But also remember, when you are praying, God is listening, when you are standing next to someone in love and support, God is there with you, and when you are overwhelmed, God's arms will enfold you and support you.

'You are in my thoughts and prayers' is not, as my colleague thought, bland and meaningless; it is a powerful and profound statement of how much the other person means to us, and how much we all mean to God.

2nd June 2023

A few weeks ago, a lovely lady came into the shop with her daughter and granddaughter, and looked through all our Sympathy cards. As she picked up different cards and read the words, her granddaughter made notes in a small notebook she was carrying. After looking at the cards, they then looked through one of the hymn books, and again, the granddaughter made notes. When they came to the counter with a couple of the cards, and a selection of Prayer Cards, the daughter smiled at me and said 'You must be wondering what we're doing?'. I had to admit that I had been a little intrigued, and she said, looking at the older lady, 'We're planning Mum's funeral'. I looked at the grandmother, very sprightly and very much alive, and was rewarded by a beaming smile. 'Yes, my funeral,' she said.

The grandmother's name was Mary, and she went on to explain that although she wasn't ill, and wasn't that old, she had recently had to arrange her sister's funeral and had had no idea where to start. She didn't know whether her sister wanted to be buried or cremated, she didn't know her favourite hymn, and she had no idea what bible passage to choose, or if her sister had had a favourite poem. On top of mourning the death of her sister, she had been faced with the stress and worry of wanting to do right by her, wanting to ensure everyone was able to remember and give thanks for her sister's life in the way her sister would have wanted, but without really knowing what that was, and she had decided that she wasn't going to put her family through the same.

Before I continue, you may be thinking that this isn't my usual sort of ramble, that I'm getting a bit morbid, but I'm not. Nor do I want this to make you sad, because in talking to Mary, I realised that in planning her funeral, she had had some wonderful conversations with her daughter, son, grandchildren, and many of her friends. They had reminisced about family holidays, planned to revisit places they hadn't been to for years, and talked about people Mary had known in her childhood, and events the family had no idea she had experienced. They had laughed at old photographs, sung songs they hadn't listened to in years, and spent a lot of time together. It had also given them the opportunity to talk about their feelings, to air long buried hurts, to heal old wounds, as well as to tell each other how much they meant, how much they were loved.

Officiating at a funeral is one of the most important things I do as your Priest. Walking with family and friends as they mourn is a privilege and a humbling experience, but it is one

197

that also makes me sad as I often hear people say 'I wish I had told them how much they meant to me', 'I wish I had talked to them about ...'. In planning her funeral, Mary was able to tell her family and friends how much they meant to her, and to tell them about her life, her feelings, her hopes and dreams for them, as well as to know how much she was loved.

Many churches offer a Funeral Planning booklet, as we do in The Valley. It is designed to allow you to tell your family and friends what you would like to happen, what hymns you like, what bible passage you want, or don't want, but I also hope it will give you the opportunity to talk. To talk to your family, to talk to your friends, to talk to me if you wish. A chance to tell each other how much you are loved, how much you mean to each other, how much you mean to the community in which you live.

Mary popped back into the shop this week to show me her funeral plan and to buy a few things she wanted to leave to her children and grandchildren, to be given to them on the day of her funeral. I hope she will be back again next year, and for many years to come, as her plans change, as her grandchildren grow, as she has great grandchildren, but if I don't see her again I can still give thanks for her, and for the opportunity she had to tell those she loves just how much they mean to her, and for the fact that when the time comes, she has given them the freedom to grieve in the confidence that she also knew how much she was loved and to do what she did every day, to celebrate life.

9th June 2023

One of the things I love about nature is its ability to surprise us. In the Rectory garden, we have shade loving plants that are thriving in full sun, a rose that is a beautiful deep red, throwing out the odd flower of a deep magenta, on the same stem as the deep red, and the biggest surprise of all, fresh asparagus, from the garden, for lunch on Christmas Day.

People are the same. We have a regular customer in the shop who, to be honest, is a bit of a grump most of the time. Our sympathy cards are never exactly what he is looking for; we don't have in stock the one book he is after, which often went out of print 20 years ago, and it is either too hot or too cold in the shop (although we usually agree with him on that one). However, every so often, he will surprise us by asking about my sister, by name, or the manager's other role as Chairman of the Prayer Book Society, and he is really interested and really engaged. He will sometimes share details as to who he is buying the card for, or why he wanted that particular book (usually for a gift), and when he does, he is charming, friendly, and frankly a joy to talk with.

But the people who surprise me most, and who in doing so make me a little ashamed of my assumptions and yes, my unconscious bias, are the ones who come in in fairly large groups, are very loud, and who leave a glorious chaos in their wake. I am talking about the Traveller Community. Now I know that there are some in that community who do not endear themselves by taking over carparks or green spaces, who leave rubbish behind, and who yes, sometimes shoplift, but as it has been said, "You can't judge the many by the actions of the few." Neither can you judge a book by its cover.

The travellers who recently came into the shop were, at first glance, all in their 20's or 30's, scantily dressed, and as I said, very loud. I'm sorry to say that their arrival did cause a couple of other customers to hastily put back the books they were looking at and scurry out of the shop, tutting as they went, but I had a wonderful 20 – 30 minutes helping them find exactly what they were looking for. At first glance, they did all look in their 20's or 30's, but then one of them called over her grandmother, who it turns out, was in her late 50's. The grandmother, whose name was Lizzie, was looking for a gift for her grandson's baptism. Cards were put on the counter, books collected from the children's section, and a wonderfully colourful rosary chosen from the jewellery cabinet. And then she said, 'Can you read me what it says in the cards, I never learnt'. There was no embarrassment, no awkwardness, and no thought that I would refuse, which of course, I didn't. We spent time deciding on whether the picture on the front or the words inside were more important; it was the words, and we agreed on the best book to help her son introduce his son to the story of Jesus.

But what surprised me, although it shouldn't have, was their knowledge of the bible, of the church, and their deep, deep faith. When I looked more closely, every one of the group, men and women, were wearing a cross or a crucifix, and a couple of them compared the rosaries they were carrying with the one they had chosen to buy. Lizzie spoke about the importance of baptism, following the example and command of Jesus, and about the sense of awe and wonder she feels every time she attends Mass. Just as with the shade loving plant that thrives in the sun, these customers showed me that we cannot and shouldn't decide on who someone is, and how someone will behave, because of their background or their way of life, and certainly not because of what we have been told about them. People are not always what they seem, or what we think they will be.

Once the decisions had been made and the chosen items purchased, Lizzie sent her children and grandchildren around the shop to put everything else back where they had found it and to restore the shop to how it had been when they arrived. They didn't get everything right, and as I said, they left a glorious chaos behind them, but their enthusiasm and eagerness were infectious, and as I tidied up after them, I did so with a smile on my face.

So I hope and pray that the next time a large group of loud, enthusiastic people come in, I will remember Lizzie and her family, and I will also remember the words God spoke to Samuel 'The Lord does not look at the things people look at. People look at the outward appearance, but the Lord looks at the heart." (1 Samuel 16: 7b)

16th June 2023

"Be kind to each other, look after each other,
don't have hate in your hearts."

The words at the top of this Ramble won't be found as a headline on the front page of any national newspaper today, but they should be. They are the words of Sinead O'Malley, mother of Grace O'Malley-Kumar, senselessly and brutally killed on Tuesday as she walked home from a night out with her friend, Barnaby Webber. They echo the words of Barnaby's mother, when speaking of the man who killed her son, "I know he will receive the retribution that he deserves; however, this evil person is just that. He is just a person. Please hold no hate that relates to any colour, sex, or religion."

These two families, who should have been preparing to welcome their children home after their first year at university, are instead preparing for their funerals. The family of Ian Coates should be organising a party to celebrate his retirement as school caretaker, but instead they are preparing for an inquest. But in their unimaginable grief, they have all spoken with love, with integrity, and with a huge amount of dignity. Through understandable tears and heart wrenching agony, they have spoken no words of hate, no words of blame.

Most newspaper headlines you will see today are full of all those things, hate, blame, accusations, and what the copy writers think, with the benefit of that wonderful thing called hindsight, should have been done, or shouldn't have been done. But what if rather than focusing on the negatives, we focused on the positives? What if rather than a message of hate, we looked for a message of love?

The words of Emma Webber and Sinead O'Malley reminded me of Gordon Wilson, whose daughter Marie died when the IRA bombed the Enniskillen Remembrance Day service in 1987, "But I bear no ill will. I bear no grudge. Dirty sort of talk is not going to bring her back to life. I will pray for these men tonight and every night." Gordon Wilson is credited, even by people within the IRA, with speeding up the peace process. He is credited with disarming the bombers, not with violence but with love and forgiveness. There are so many examples of the families of murder victims forgiving their killers, so many people who would rather remember their loved ones for the lives they led, rather than the way they died.

I know, and agree, that we need to hold politicians, civil servants, doctors, scientists, police officers, everyone in authority and power, to account. We need to know that they will learn from the past, that they, and we, will learn from their, and other peoples, mistakes, but isn't it as important, or even more important, to look to what we can learn from ordinary people, people like us. Emma, Sinead, Gordon, and oh so many others, didn't seek the limelight, and would have done everything in their power to stop what happened to their children if they could, but their reaction to tragedy is an example to us all. I don't know if the families of the Nottingham victims are people of faith. I do know that Gordon Wilson was a committed and faithful Christian, but whether they are people of faith or people of none, they are living examples of the message at the heart of Jesus' teaching 'Love one another', and Paul's message to the Ephesians '"Be kind and compassionate to one another, forgiving each other, just as in Christ, God forgave you."

Mirah Gomah, whose son David was stabbed to death in 2020, said of his killers, "You have killed my son. You butchered him - he did nothing at all. I forgive you."

If she can forgive, if the families of the Nottingham victims can speak of holding no hate in our hearts, how much easier should it be for us to forgive past hurts, to forgive words spoken in haste. It isn't easy to forgive, I know, but when we look at all our blessings, when we look at all that is good in the world, when we see all the people who are working for peace, working to feed the hungry and clothe the naked, working for a better life for the poor, the lost and the lonely, and when we stop focusing on all that is bad, we, along with the Nottingham families, can remember the words of Desmond Tutu after the end of Apartheid 'We have lived through our nightmare. You will too'.

"Be kind to each other, look after each other, don't have hate in your hearts."

28th July 2023

It isn't very often that the people of the Mediterranean envy us our weather, but they are at the moment. It's also hard to believe, as I sit and look out at another damp and dull day, a 'typical British summer', that this time last year I was rambling about the heatwave that had hit us, and the wildfires breaking out across Britain.

July is, according to the experts, the hottest month the world has known since records began, but the record isn't expected to stand for long. The hottest temperate recorded so far is 48.8 degrees, hotter than the temperature most of us do our washing on, and although it is a long way from the 56.7 degrees recorded in Death Valley, California, in 1913, the frequency of extreme temperatures, and the area those temperatures cover, are increasing at an alarming rate, faster than even the experts predicted.

The wildfires in Greece and Rhodes may have hit the headlines primarily because of the tourists who have, in some cases, had to run from their hotels with just the clothes they have on, grabbing passports, credit cards, and cash as they leave, but for the locals, the impact will last a lot longer. Homes and businesses have been destroyed, and will take years to rebuild, if ever, and sadly, lives have also been lost as firefighters and pilots battle the extreme heat and the raging flames.

In Spain, farmers are out in the fields at 2 am, avoiding the heat of the day, to plant crops they have very little hope will survive because of the lack of water and the extreme heat, while tourist attractions in Greece, Italy, and Spain are closed during the hottest part of the day and volunteers hand out bottles of water by the thousands, to both locals and tourists.

Humans are, generally, pretty good at adapting to changes in temperature and rainfall, with farmers looking at drought resistance crops, new ways of farming, or even the introduction of crops that 30 or 40 years ago were only grown in the Med, or even in Arica. We can change our habits, and even our work, maybe in future, adopting the midday siesta, starting work earlier to avoid the heat, and wearing thinner, cooler clothes. But for the rest of creation, adaptation is a slower process, often taking several generations, and the loss of habitat, or even minute changes in the eco system they need to survive, can lead to extinction.

This time last year, as I reflected on the effect of Global Warming and Climate Change on our country, I wrote about the Church of England's Five Marks of Mission, and

209

especially the Fifth Mark - 'To strive to safeguard the integrity of creation, and sustain and renew the life of the earth'.

In 1623, John Donne, regarded by many as one of England's greatest poets, coined the phrase 'No man is an Island entire of itself'. The quote doesn't come from one of his poems, but from a sermon he preached as Dean of St Paul's Cathedral. Donne's focus was on humankind, how we are all connected to each other, and how we, even the most solitary, need other people to survive and thrive. I can't help but wonder, if he were alive today, whether Donne would change his words and his meaning. If he climbed into the pulpit today, would his words not be 'No man is an island', but instead 'Mankind, humankind, is not an island, entire of itself', because humankind cannot survive without the rest of creation.

As we cut down rain forests and build on flood plans, as we reclaim land from the sea, to grow more and more crops and provide more and more houses, we are contributing to the loss of species and of habitats that are vital to the survival of not just the animals, the flora and fauna, that make those areas home, we are contributing to the loss of major parts of the food chain. Without the plankton in the sea, the worms and the bugs on the earth, we are in danger of turning the whole of creation, and our existence, into a worldwide game of Jenga. Pull out too many of the lower building blocks of life, and the whole thing may come tumbling down.

John Donne spoke of our reliance on each other, of our need for community and support. Today, we need to look at what we can do, in our own small way, to offer support and survival to the rest of creation, to sustain and renew the life of the earth because we need it, as much as it needs us.

1st September 2023

This week, someone in the shop asked me to order a book for them called 'What would Jesus tweet?' (Thankfully written before Twitter became X, because I have no idea what a post on X is called! Anyway, I digress.) The book contains over 200 quotes from the Gospels, putting Jesus' message into the then Twitter format of 140 words. (I admit I'm not a twitter user and so have no idea if that still holds). Each quote does come with the bible reference so readers can find and read the full passage if they want, but it is designed, as so much of our lives are these days, as a quick win, as an instant gratification. The person who asked for the book admitted he wanted to be able to quote the Bible at church, without having to actually read the Bible! He didn't want the whole picture; he didn't want the whole story. I must admit I had to bite my tongue to stop the reply that sprang into my mind!

But it got me thinking, what would Jesus do if he were alive today? How would he communicate? In the musical Jesus Christ Superstar, Judas challenges Jesus, at the foot of the cross, 'If you'd come today, you would have reached a whole nation. Israel in 4 BC had no mass communication'. The mass communication he is referring to is TV and

212

newspapers, because the musical was written before the invention of the World Wide Web, before emails, and before mobile phones. If Jesus came today, his every move, every healing, every quiet time, would be splashed not only on our TV screen and front pages but would go viral on social media. Judgement on who he is would not just come from the leaders of the nations, and his own disciples, but from anyone with a computer or mobile phone, anyone who had heard a soundbite, or seen an image of a miracle. Would that be a good thing, he could reach the whole world at one time, or a bad thing, in that it would lose the personal touch.

Mass communication, modern communication, has its benefits, and I use text and emails as much as the next person, but just like the customer who wanted the Bible in bite size pieces, it can lead to us missing the bigger picture, and more importantly, missing the human element. In wanting to be able to quote Jesus' words without knowing the circumstances in which they were said, without knowing who they were addressed to, our customer will miss so much of Jesus' teaching, because it wasn't all about words, it was about action, it was about welcoming in the outsider, helping the poor and the feeding the hungry.

When Jesus fed the 5000, he preached to them first, and what he said had to be relayed back through the crowd, strangers speaking to each other, from different backgrounds, different countries, even different faiths. The personal element, the face-to-face encounters, broke down the barriers that in our modern world are sometimes strengthened by social media, by sound bites, by tweets. Knowing what happened before, and after, is just as important as knowing the event, the saying, itself.

'Love one another. As I have loved you, so you must love one another' (John 13: 33), is one of the most well-known and often quoted sayings of Jesus, and is front and centre in 'What would Jesus Tweet'. But surely its message, its meaning, is strengthened when we know that Jesus has just humbled himself and washed the feet of his disciples, against every social convention, in an act of service. Surely its importance is heightened when we know that this takes place the night before Jesus died, the ultimate act of love and sacrifice.

As social media becomes more and more powerful, as lives are defined, and sometimes destroyed, by sound bites and tweets, we need to look beyond. We need to look at the before and after, we need to understand the lives of the people involved, and we need to know the whole story. In the 21st Century we are Jesus' mass communication, in what we do, what we say, and how we live, and I pray that we will live up to the greatest message, 'Love one another' without judgement, without condemnation, breaking down barriers and being his true disciples, and seeing, and being, the bigger picture.

8th September 2023

This week I've been following a little book of meditations based on the writings of Julian of Norwich, the 14th century mystic. The meditations are based on her book 'Revelations of Divine Love', the first book ever published by a woman. The first meditation reflected on Julian's three wishes, or as she referred to them, 'the three graces'. She firstly wished to experience, as though present, Christ's Passion (His death on the cross), the second was to experience a bodily sickness (so that she could understand the pain and suffering he experienced), and thirdly she wished for three wounds (to carry the marks of the nails). Now, even in the 14th century, these were extreme and unusual wishes, which Julian herself acknowledged, but she did, in her lifetime, experience all of them.

Reading the meditation got me thinking about what my three wishes would be, in my faith and in my life, and also wondering what others would wish for. Now, Google is a wonderful thing, and after much searching, I found a piece about a small radio station in America which had run a survey amongst its listeners as to what they would wish for if they found Aladdin's Lamp. Once they had taken out some of the very specific wishes, for a particular car or holiday, the wishes fell into three categories - personal wealth, personal/family health, and world peace. More in-depth analysis found that the majority of people who had wished for wealth had actually wished for 'enough money to retire/buy a house/send the kids to University'. Only a few people had actually wanted huge wealth, had wanted to win the Lottery, or to become a millionaire. Those who had wished for personal/family health had done so wishing for a long and fulfilled life, for them, their children, and grandchildren. The wish for world peace speaks for itself, and I'm sure it is one we all agree with.

In reading the results of a survey done amongst people I don't know, on the other side of the world, I was surprised but also heartened by the fact that they wished for what I would call a contented life. They didn't want the wealth, it is imagined we all desire; they didn't want huge success for their children; they wanted enough. Enough money to not have to worry about the next bill, and enough good health, for them and their family, to be able to enjoy all that life has to offer. I don't know about you, but I have to say I agree with them, to a point. A contented life, with enough money, good health, and world peace, would fulfil most people's wishes for their life, but not for their faith. To have a fulfilled life in faith, I need to turn to our own saint, St Richard of Chichester, and

217

the quote at the top of this ramble, containing his three wishes, his three prayers, and make them my own.

'O Dear Lord, three things I pray, to see thee more clearly, to love thee more dearly, to follow thee more nearly, day by day. Amen'.

29th September 2023

This Sunday (1ˢᵗ October) we will be celebrating Harvest Festival. It is a time to give thanks for all that God has given us in creation, and to share some of our blessings with those less fortunate by bringing donations for the Chichester Food Bank.

It is also the time when the Manouch household reviews how successful, or not, we have been with our harvest over the year. We keep a record of all the produce we have grown in the garden, and compare it with previous years, to decide what works and what doesn't, and to begin planning for next year's crops. I say we, but really I mean my sister, as she does most of the planting and tending, and I just help with the harvest, and of course, enjoy the fruits of her labour. I won't bore you with all the details, but simply to say that we had a bumper year of beans, courgettes, raspberries, and grapes (1.8 kg, the best year ever!). It was an OK year for rhubarb, strawberries, asparagus, and potatoes, but we lost most of our tomatoes to blight! We also harvested a lot of blackberries, but can take no credit for them as they grow wild in the Rectory hedge! Some of what we grow is a success every year, the beans especially see us through to Christmas, once blanched and frozen, whilst other crops are badly hit by the unseasonal changes in temperature and rain fall, just as are the crops in the fields around us in the Valley. Climate Change can also bring some unexpected bonus', with the unseasonably warm weather last Autumn/Winter giving us fresh Asparagus from the garden for Christmas Day.

The thing about nature, about creation, is that it adapts. It may take some time, and it may mean we no longer have the fruit and vegetables we are used to, when we are used to them, but we will still have enough food for everyone, if we want there to be. If we stop the food waste that clogs up land fill. If we stop wasting water and resources to produce out of season products. If we eat seasonally, it is not only healthier for us, but also for the world around us. I know the farmers are constantly looking at what needs to be grown when, and where, and adapting their practises to meet the needs not just of their customers but also of the world around them, and we need to do the same.

One of the highlights of our holiday in Portugal was visiting a couple of Quintas, the estates that border the Douro Valley and produce the grapes for the wine, and more importantly, the Port, synonymous with the region. Port makers are not allowed to water their crops. The vines that produce the grapes for the amazing White, Tawny, and Red Ports have to fend for themselves, whatever the weather. Because of that, some of their roots are 7 metres long, reaching down deep into the earth to get the nourishment they need. Some of the vines we saw were over 100 years old, and when the time comes to replace them, large mechanical diggers are needed to excavate the root systems. The Port producers have also had to adapt, harvesting slightly earlier than they have in the past because of the changes in climate, but they, like to vines, have done so successfully.

On Sunday, we will be singing some of the classic, and favourite, Harvest hymns, We Plough the Fields and Scatter, For the Beauty of the Earth, All Creatures of our God and King, and of course, Come, ye thankful people come. We will be singing in grateful thanks, and recognition, of all that God has provided for us, but also promising to be stewards, to be caretakers, of that gift, of creation. God, our Maker, doth provide for our wants to be supplied, so it says in the harvest hymn. It is up to us to decide if we want to share what he has provided, and if we want to ensure his gifts are there for future generations. It is up to us to decide if we want to adapt, to rethink, to ensure that future generations can also enjoy the fruits of God's harvest.

13th October 2023

I'm sure many of you will be able to sympathise with me when I say that this week I haven't known if I am coming or going! It has been so busy with meetings and visits and work that sometimes I have had to just stop, refocus, and remember who I am going to see, what we're going to be talking about, and panic over whether I have the right paperwork. Thankfully, all has gone well, and I was in the right place, at the right time, with everything I needed.

However, there have been two meetings this week that I have missed, and both of them were on Wednesday. They were my morning and evening meetings with God, in the form of Morning and Evening Prayer. Now that isn't to say that I didn't pray on Wednesday. I prayed before each of my meetings, and I prayed at the end of the day, but I really missed the 20 minutes or so at the start of the day when I offered to God all that I was to do, asked for his guidance, his support, and the courage to face all the day would bring. I missed my time in the evening when I look back on the day, give thanks for all the blessings I received, pray for all the people I had met, and ask forgiveness for things I had done, or not done, things I had said or not said.

It is so easy in a busy life to think that time with God is something we can 'put off' to another day, or another time, because after all God is always there, he isn't going anywhere, he won't ask us to call back when he's less busy, and we never get his 'out of office'. But time with God, whether in formal prayer or on a walk in the country, or just sitting down with a cup of coffee, is about more than asking him for help, or thanking him for something good that has happened. It is also a time for us to focus on us.

A busy life often means that our time and energy are always directed to what we have to do next, the next task, the next meeting, the next day. Time with God, or just time 'being' with ourselves, means that we can look at what the Diocese of Gloucester calls the Wow, the Ow, and the Now moments of our day and our life. Now the Diocese uses the metaphor in their thinking about Spiritual Growth, but stopping for a few minutes every day and thinking about the wows, ows, and nows of our life is also good for our mental and physical wellbeing.

Although it may be hard at times to think about a wow moment, when something so beautiful, or good, or breath-taking happens that we are stopped in our tracks, Wow moments can happen in small ways too. A kestrel hovering over a field, a child laughing as they play on the swings, a stranger paying you a compliment. These are all wow moments because they are unexpected and bring a smile to our faces, and a little lift in our spirits. These are moments to treasure, to savour, and to bring before God as blessings.

Ow moments may be easier to identify. They are the moments when something happens that again stops us in our tracks, but because they have caused us pain or sadness. We get bad news from the doctor. We say something cruel to someone, often unintentionally, and see the hurt in their eyes. Someone says something cruel or hurtful to us. These are the moments that we need to think about, reflect on, and acknowledge, not hide away from, so they eat away at our sense of self-worth. They are also the moments to bring before God in prayers of help, healing, and maybe forgiveness.

And what about the Now moments? Well, 10 minutes with God or quietly with a cup of coffee is a now moment. A break in the busyness of the day, when you stop and have a moment of stillness, when you can take a long, slow, deep breath and relax. They are also moments to treasure because they are the moments that give you the energy, the focus, and the clarity to give your best. There are moments to thank God for.

The next time I am so busy that I don't think I have time for God is the time that I know I need to stop, step back, and give myself time to see the Wow, the Ow, and the Now of my day, and offer it all to God in prayer. Then I will be ready to face whatever the rest of the day will bring.

27th October 2023

8 pm, Saturday 28th October, has been in my diary for quite a while. It was something I had been looking forward to, and I had the evening all planned. A couple of bottles of lager, the rare treat of a take away, and my sister and I would settle down to watch England play whoever in the Rugby Union World Cup Final. Except now it isn't going to happen. A 78th minute penalty from South Africa in the semi-final put an end to my plans. I'm sure it will be a good game tomorrow, but I won't be watching it.

With just 2 minutes to go, Handre Pollard, the South African Fly-half, put an end to all my hopes, and the hopes of millions of other England Rugby fans. I have to admit that I had put the entry in my diary more in hope than expectation. Very few people expected England to get as far as they did. We hoped they'd make it out of the group matches, but on recent form that wasn't certain, and then we hoped they'd make the semi's, but again, not certain, and then we hoped against hope that the final beckoned, but that final hope was a hope to far. But still, we can take comfort from the fact that they now have the basis of a great team that may one day emulate the team of 2003 and bring the Webb Ellis Cup home again.

Now, you may be wondering where I am going with this Ramble, especially if you're not a rugby fan, but thinking about events over the past couple of weeks, and not just the rugby, has got me thinking about hope and what it really means. In his first letter to the Corinthians, St Paul says 'And now these three remain; faith, hope, and love, and the greatest of these is love' (1 Cor 13: 13). For some people, the inclusion of hope seems a little odd. Faith, yes of course, and love, absolutely, but what place does the slightly random nature of hope have to do with God and with faith.

If you look in any dictionary, they all say pretty much the same thing about hope. It is a wish or desire for something good to happen, or for something bad not to happen. 'I hope I can get tickets for the show I want to see', 'I hope the car will start', 'I hope England make the final!'. But the Biblical definition of hope is a little different. In the bible, hope isn't a wish or desire; it is an expectation with certainty that God will do what he says, that he will always be there, always listening, always comforting. Dictionary hope is a wish or desire, biblical hope is a certainty or guarantee.

In the anonymous letter to the Hebrews, the writer says 'Now faith is confidence in what we hope for and assurance about what we do not see' (Hebrews 11:1). This is the bedrock of faith, confidence in what we hope for, and assurance of what we do not see. We can have faith because we have hope, and we have hope because we have faith. Faith filled hope is a kind of 'in spite of' hope. In spite of what we see, in spite of what is going on, in spite of what a situation looks like, we can have hope because we have faith. We have faith in a God who cannot lie, we have faith in a Son who died for us, and we have faith in the Holy Spirit who is our support and comforter. The situation may not change immediately, we may not get an answer to our prayers when, and how, we want them, but because we have hope, faith, and love, we can face the challenges of daily life with confidence and certainty that we do not face them alone.

3rd November 2023

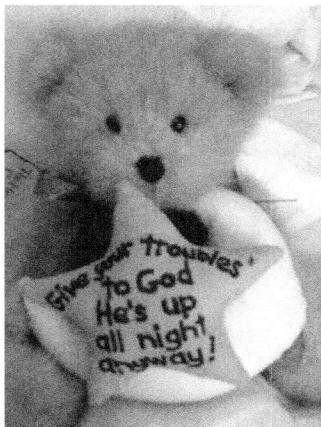

One of the programmes we watch every week at the Rectory is Saving Lives at Sea, following RNLI crews from around the country as they battle the elements to help people in trouble around our coast, and also on some of our lakes and rivers. The men and women who answer their pagers at all hours often don't know what they are being called to as they launch their boats, setting out prepared for anything, waiting for more information as they speed their way through often rough seas and treacherous conditions. Last night's programme included a yacht taking on water, a man caught out by the incoming tide, and the rescue of a deer!

The reaction of those rescued is always relief and gratitude, but also often embarrassment. As they are pulled from the sea, or carried from one vessel to another, the RNLI crews hear 'I'm sorry' as often as they hear 'Thank you'. (I don't know how the deer felt, but as we saw it released back into the wild, it skipped away happily without a backward glance).

But why do those rescued feel embarrassed? Well, yes, sometimes they haven't taken the precautions they should, haven't checked the tide times, aren't wearing the right clothes, but I wonder if it is also because none of us like to admit we can't cope, don't like to admit we need help. In the 21st Century, we are all supposed to be self-sufficient, we're supposed to be in control, we're supposed to be able to handle whatever life throws at us. But that isn't how we are made. We are people who need people, we are people who are at our best when we are in community and fellowship with others, when we work together. The men and women of the RNLI know this. They don't launch with just one person on the boat; they don't send just one person to help a stricken yacht or stranded deer; they work as a team, each using their particular skills and gifts to benefit the whole.

But there are people who don't go out in the boats, don't answer the pagers, who are vital to the success of each launch. They are the ones who stay at home; they are the wives, husbands, partners, and children of the RNLI crews who make it possible for them to drop everything and run

230

when called. Several of the crew members made it clear on last night's programme that without that support at home and at work, they couldn't do what they do. We all need someone, be it family or friend, who we know is there for us no matter what. Someone who doesn't judge us for not being prepared, for not being able to cope.

But for people of faith, we also always have the constant, non-judgemental, ever ready and available help of God, if we ask for it. Just as with those rescued by the RNLI, my prayers often include as many 'I'm sorry', as they do 'thank you', but also just as the lifeboat crews reply 'don't apologise, that's what we're here for', so does God. Yes, we need to admit to God, and to ourselves, when we haven't lived up to our calling as Christians, haven't done all we should, haven't been all we should be, but we don't need to fear God's reaction, don't need to fear admitting our failings, don't need to worry about not being able to cope on our own.

The picture at the top of this Ramble is of a teddy bear I was given by a friend while I was in training for Ordination. It is a reminder that God is constant, that God is always there, that God is ready to hear our cries for help, ready to offer comfort, support, and a guiding hand back to safety. All we need to do is ask.

8th December 2023

One of our favourite programmes on TV, which finished its season this week, is Portrait Artist of the Year, on Sky Arts. What I find fascinating is seeing how 3 artists, presented with the same person to paint, can come up with 3 totally different images. One may go for a full-length portrait, tackling the difficulties of hands and including lots of background. Another will produce what seems a mash up of different colours and shapes that, close up, looks like a bit of a mess, but from a distance is a, sometimes, amazing reflection of the sitter. A third will, hopefully for me anyway, go for a 'traditional' portrait of head and shoulders, producing a painting that is instantly recognisable and captures a twinkle in the eye, or a gentle smile.

It's said that beauty is in the eye of the beholder, and more often than not, I have disagreed with the judge's final decision as to which painting is best, which painter is worth sending through to the next round. It is also rare for me to agree with the overall winner, but not this year. This year, the winner (who happens to come from Worthing) produced stunning portraits, in the traditional style, and now has her final painting hanging in the National Portrait Gallery.

Thinking about how I see things differently to the judges (and often to my sister) in a painting competition got me thinking about how often we fail to see things from the other side, from the other person's perceptive. How often do we think that we are right because of what we know, believe, or have always done?

The picture at the top of the Ramble is often used in offices, classrooms, and even within church communities, as an aid to conflict resolution. The two figures arguing over which number is represented are both right, and both wrong; it just depends on which side you stand on as to whether you see a 6 or a 9.

Christmas is, sadly, often a time when individuals, families, and even churches, disagree over what is the 'right' thing to do. Should the Christmas decorations go up on 1st December, Advent Sunday, or Christmas Eve? Tradition says Christmas Eve, but for families, clergy, and those who work long hours, often in shifts, it is more a case of 'when do I have the time?'. Should the candles in the Advent Wreath be purple, pink, and white, or red and white? Each church will have its own tradition, and there is no right or wrong answer, but major rows can arise if the 'wrong' colours are used. In St Olav's Bookshop, we have a few customers who tell us we are wrong to sell Christmas cards before the beginning of Advent, as we are cashing in on the commercialisation of Christmas. Now putting aside the argument that if we didn't sell cards when everybody else does, we would lose out on so many sales we wouldn't survive, we know that for many peoples, struggling with money worries, being able to spread the cost of Christmas over 2 or 3 months is a blessing. A couple of packs of cards a month, a couple of presents a month, won't break the bank, but will mean their family has a wonderful Christmas.

As we get closer to the Big Day, and the stress, worry, and busyness increase, I pray that we will all be able to see 'the other side' of an argument, a disagreement, or a situation. Yes, there are some things that have a simple right and wrong answer, but not as many as we think, because there is usually a different point of view, a different perspective, a different tradition. Let us make this Advent and Christmas a time when we all try to see things from the other side, when we understand the other person's point of view. If the whole world would step into the other person's shoes, the other person's life, if only for a few minutes, and see things from their point of view, then maybe conflict would end and the world would be a better place, the world would be a peace filled place.

26th January 2024

I've been taking advantage, over the past couple of months, of wet and windy Thursdays to sort out the books in my office. I had 10 shelves full to overflowing and am now down to 5 1/2, with 6 boxes of surplus books ready to go to either Age UK, or more likely, the second-hand section in St Olav's. I know it will look less impressive when on a zoom call with the diocese, or other clergy, but I also know that others will be able to benefit from all the books I no longer need or want.

The books I am passing on are ones I used for essay writing during training, or which I needed during my curacy, but I know I will (probably) never read them again. There are also some I bought with every good intention of reading, but which now don't have the same appeal, don't fit in with where I am now, and so they are also on their way out.

But the greatest joy was in 'rediscovering' books I had forgotten I had, books like Kingdom of Fools by Nick Page, A Journey into God by Delia Smith, and Falling Upwards by Richard Rohr. These, and so many others, have played a huge part in my life and faith journey and now sit on a separate shelf ready for me to reread and enjoy all over again. I had so many books on my shelves, double depth in some cases, that the important ones, the ones I should have been reading, just got lost.

It got me thinking about other parts of my life where I get overwhelmed by the sheer volume of what I have to do that I miss out on the small but important things that not only bring me joy, but also bring me closer to God and closer to the people around me. It also got me reflecting on how my bookcases could be said to reflect my thinking. Things that happened in the past that caused me pain, things that I regret doing, or not doing, events that happened 10 or 20 years ago that I still think about, and sometimes still worry about, all of these can crowd out or drown the important things, the things I should be focusing on.

I think we all, to a certain extent, spend time on the 'what if's' of life. What if that hadn't happened, what if I had chosen that path, what if I (they) hadn't said or done that? These thoughts, regrets, and sadnesses can overwhelm us and stop us from seeing, feeling, experiencing, and remembering the good times, the times of joy, the times when things went right, not wrong, the times we were uplifted, not brought down low.

In sorting out my books, there were some I put straight back on the shelf, some I put straight into the box to go, and some

I put to one side as 'maybes', maybe keep, maybe go. I then revisited them and made myself make a decision. As the saying goes, if in doubt, throw it out, or the mantra for decluttering, 'if it isn't useful, pretty, or brings you joy, it's time to get rid of it'. It will be a much harder task to sort out my thinking, to be able to say to those thoughts that dwell on the past 'it's time to go', but I am determined to do it. Determined to park them in a box marked unwanted and to focus on the thoughts that are useful, or bring me, or others, joy.

The words below are on a small card I was given when I left my former parish, and which I rediscovered as a bookmark in one of the books now on the 'must read again' shelf. It is a card I will carry with me, and they are words I will try to live by.

I Am

I was regretting the past and fearing the future.
Suddenly my Lord was speaking
'My name is I AM'
He paused; I waited; he continued

When you live in the past,
with its mistakes and regrets,

it is hard. I am not there:

My name is not I was.

When you live in the future,

with its problems and fears,

it is hard. I am not there:

My name is not I will be.

When you live in the moment,

It is not hard. I am here,

My name is I AM.

2nd February 2024

On Monday night, I didn't come home so much on a wing and a prayer as 3 good tyres and a prayer! Having been to a lovely service in Compton to welcome the new Vicar in the Octagon Benefice, I set off for home in high spirits with wonderful music still ringing in my ears. It wasn't too last long! As I rounded a blind bend in the road, I hit what can only be described as a chasm sized pot hole, which jolted the car so much my sat nav flew out of its holder and my handbag jumped off the seat beside me. It wasn't long before I realised I had an almost, if not completely, flat tyre. Now I know that the advice is not to drive on a flat but I was in the middle of nowhere, with no houses in sight, and more importantly no mobile phone signal, and so I soldiered on and by the time I did see lights I decided that the damage was done and I might as well just keep going.

Having made it home safely, I then spent a sleepless night ignoring all my own advice and last week's Ramble, going over and over what I should have done, and then the worst-case scenarios. Had I damaged the wheel, had I cracked the suspension, how much would it cost to fix, and would it even be worth it, and could I get a hire car for the weekend? Oh, and on top of that, the damaged tyre had only been fitted 3 days before Christmas following a puncture caused by shards of glass! All in all, it seemed like a hopeless situation.

But it needed to be sorted, and so on Tuesday I phoned the RAC and while waiting for them, got recommendations for garages which offered vehicle recovery and checked out the availability of hire cars. Knowing I wouldn't be a high priority because I was at home, I phoned work, took the day off, and spent the morning pottering. I did some tidying up and then blitzed my personal email account to unsubscribe from unwanted weekly, and sometimes daily, updates about items I didn't want, or events I had no intention of going to. I also put together a list in my head of all the people I would need to contact to cancel meetings or social events, yes, I really was going all out on a worst-case scenario. But even as I waited for what I thought would be bad news there were wonderful and uplifting moments as friends who had seem my appeal for garage advice offered to pick me up if I was stranded, and while waiting for the RAC at the end of the drive (his sat nav had sent him to the wrong place) I was offered lifts or help by both neighbours and passers-by.

So finally, lovely Lee from the RAC arrived, cheerful, friendly, and totally understanding of my desire to get home the night before. Within minutes, he reassured me that no, I hadn't damaged the wheel, the suspension was fine, and I didn't need to get the car picked up and taken to a garage because he could recommend mobile tyre fitters that could come to me. Twenty minutes after he left, I had booked a tyre fitting for Thursday (another friendly young man called Danny), phoned my sister to tell her the better-than-expected news, and settled down for an unexpected afternoon off of reading, chilling, and taking advantage of some quiet time with God.

As I sat reflecting on the day's events, I was reminded of Jesus' words in the Sermon on the Mount 'So do not worry about tomorrow, for tomorrow will bring worries of its own. Today's trouble is enough for today' (Matthew 6: 34). If only I had heeded that the day before, if only I had gone to bed on Monday not only thanking God for my safe arrival home but putting aside all the what ifs, and leaving until the next day all of the things that were for the next day. I would have had a better night's sleep, I would have been less stressed in the morning, and I would have looked at what happened, and what might happen, in a clearer light.

We all have to think about tomorrow, we all have to plan for eventualities, but we don't need to let them overtake or drown out the positive, uplifting, and amazing experiences

242

of today. And as we all discovered, or rediscovered, during lockdowns and beyond, no matter what we are going through, there are always people around who will help, support, and reassure us, and we can always rely on God to comfort and uphold us, whether on a wing, or a tyre, and a prayer.

16th February 2024

I'm currently reading a fascinating book called 'Cold Case Christianity' by J Warner Wallace, in which a former cold case murder detective investigates the evidence for God and for Jesus' life and ministry, and in the process moved from being a committed atheist to becoming a committed and devout Christian.

That Jesus lived on earth is not in doubt, after all, even Roman writers of the time, with no reason to support what they considered outlandish claims, record that Jesus existed, and that he had a huge and devoted following. But what about who he is and what he did? Well, as in a real cold case, the detective goes back to the earliest evidence, and especially the earliest eye witness accounts, the Gospels, and does what I suspect very few of us have ever done, he forensically investigated every line, every event, every place. I'm not going to go into all the details about what he discovered, but I have been reflecting on what he didn't find, and what I suspect most of us realised without realising it, if you know what I mean. Nowhere in the Gospels, nor indeed anywhere in the New Testament, does anyone say what Jesus looked like! Did he have a beard, was his hair long or short, black or brown, were his eyes brown, blue, green, or black? We don't know, and it doesn't matter.

Unlike today, when any report of an event will come with details of what the person involved looked like, and probably even what clothes they were wearing, to the eye witnesses of Jesus' life and ministry, what he looked like or what accent he had, were, and are, unimportant details. Now some have argued that the lack of such detail was because they were recording the facts for a small, local, community who were all from the same cultural background and who all spoke and indeed dressed the same as Jesus had, but in fact by the time the Gospels were being written down their audience had spread across the whole of the known world, from the Middle East to Rome, from Spain to Africa. So why didn't anyone think to tell us what Jesus looked like? Well, from my point of view, I wonder if it was not only because compared to what he said and did, his hair colour was unimportant, but also because of Jesus' message. Love one another as I have loved you – unconditionally, without judgement, without prejudice. Don't see what someone looks like on the surface, at their skin colour, their hair style, their clothes, but look inside them, see Jesus in everyone.

Because we don't know what Jesus actually looked like, we are free to see him as we want to see him, and to represent him in art, sculpture, and statues as being one with us, whatever our race or culture. The image at the top of the Ramble shows just some of the ways Jesus is represented around the world, and all of them are inspiring and devotional images, all of them are a true image of Jesus, Son of God, Son of Man, because they show Jesus as one with us, whoever we are, wherever we are from. What does Jesus look like? He looks like the next person we meet, the shop assistant, the bus driver, the teacher, and we should treat them as Jesus would, love one another as I have loved you.

8th March 2024

Thank you - This week, a young man, in his 20s, walked into the Age UK charity shop and handed my sister a packet of biscuits with a simple 'Thank you'. As she racked her brain to try and remember when she had met him before, he continued and explained that his grandfather, and indeed his whole family, have received a lot of help and support from Age UK and he wanted to thank the people at the coal face, the people who helped raise the funds that allowed them to run all their activities and support groups. As he left, he said, 'It's not much, I'm afraid, but thank you again'. As my sister said, the biscuits were nice, but the thank you was priceless.

Thank you - Have you ever held the door open for someone who has sailed through without a word or a glance? Did it frustrate you as much as it does me? Now, if it's a young mum struggling with a pushchair, children, and bags of shopping, then maybe it's understandable, but I find they are the ones who nearly always say thank you, and often the children do too. And when they do, it brings a smile to my face and puts a spring in my step. On the other hand, when there is no acknowledgement, no thank you, no smile, I admit to sometimes saying a slightly sarcastic 'you're welcome' under my breath and being a bit grumpy for a few minutes.

Thank you - At the end of the day, it is good to look back over all that has happened and find the things to thank God for, and there is always something. It can be as simple as the car starting to get you to the shops or allowing you to visit friends. It can be as important as a child or grandchild getting their first job. It can be the warmth of the sun after days of rain, or the first sign of life in the garden. It can be a simple packet of biscuits from a stranger.

Thank you - There is so much that we can be grateful for, so much that we can celebrate, so many people who through small acts, make a huge difference to us and to our communities, so much we need to say thank you for. As we prepare to celebrate Mothering Sunday this weekend, let's make sure we take every opportunity to thank everyone who has made a difference to us, be it our families, our friends, the person behind the counter in the newsagents, or the driver of the local bus.

The biscuits were nice, but the thank you was priceless.

15th March 2024

This week saw the 30th anniversary of the first women being ordained as priests in the Church of England. The fact that it didn't make huge headlines was, to some, a disappointment, but to me it is a sign of hope. Hope that soon the prefix 'female' will no longer be applied to priests, as it is no longer applied to police officers, doctors, judges, teachers, soldiers, in fact, any other profession.

The reality of how women are still viewed by some in the church, and in wider society, was brought home to me during my training for ordination. I was on a train to Canterbury for a week long residential just after Easter, and as I usually do, I struck up a conversation with the person sitting opposite me. When I told him where I was going, and why, his response was 'Oh, you're training to be a female priest!'. Smiling, and a little tongue in cheek and a little exasperated, I replied 'No, I'm training to be a priest. I've been doing the female bit since the day I was born'.

Now, before any of you wonder if I am going to go into a rant against those who cannot, will not, accept the ordination of women, I'm not. I don't agree with their arguments, nor accept some of their 'logic, but I do, in love and faith, respect their views and work with them as far as I can. In fact, some within the church who do not accept my status as priest are amongst the most supportive in the practical aspects of ministry, they just won't receive either Holy Communion or a blessing from me.

Some look to St Paul to support their argument against women speaking in church, leading worship, or even having a voice of their own, because he has got a bit of a reputation as a misogynist, and I have to say I used to share that view. But then I did more reading, and had a great Biblical Studies tutor, Simon, who was a huge fan of St Paul and showed us a different side. Yes, Paul can seem to be a bit down on women sometimes, but Simon had one verse that he went back to again and again to show us Paul's true message, and it is a message that can be found in all his letters if we look for it. It is, however, at its loudest and clearest in his letter to the Galatians, 'There is neither Jew nor Gentile, neither slave nor free, nor is there male and female, for you are all one in Christ Jesus.' (Galatians 3: 28).

We are all one in Christ Jesus. It doesn't matter what gender, race, skin colour, age, or occupation, we are all one in Christ Jesus. We are equally loved, all equally valued, and all endowed with gifts and blessings. They may not be the same gifts, we may not have the same blessings, but that doesn't make one better than another; it doesn't mean one is loved by God more than another.

On the 13th of May, there is a service in Chichester Cathedral to celebrate the 30th anniversary of the Ordination of Women, and prior to that, there will be an exhibition during April of female priests from our diocese. I have never attended any celebrations before, as I didn't want to join in the 'separation' of one group from another. I will, however, be attending this year because I hope it will be the last one. I hope it will be the last time we need to bring female clergy together to remind them of St Paul's words, you are all one in Christ Jesus.

I am immensely grateful, and in awe, of the women who fought for years to give me and my colleagues the joy and privilege of serving in the priesthood, including women from this parish, but I hope and pray that they would agree with me that the ultimate sign of their success is when 'female priest' is no longer seen as unusual and worthy of comment. When a woman standing behind the altar is accepted in the same way as a woman holding a gavel, or a scalpel, or sadly a gun. So, thank you to them, thank you to the women who suffered mental and physical abuse in the fight for equality, and thank you to all of you for accepting me as your priest.

251

And I pray that our children and grandchildren will grow up to adulthood in a world where there is no distinction made in any walk of life, because of gender, race, colour, or creed, but all are seen as one in Christ Jesus, and all are loved as He loves us.

22nd March 2024

This morning, I had the joy of welcoming the pupils, staff, and parents from West Dean School into St Andrews Church for a Palm Friday/Sunday service. The children and teachers processed to the church through the village, waving palm branches and singing, following a wonderful pony taking on the role of the donkey. The service was full of songs, readings, and prayers, and we blessed Easter Gardens and saw beautiful crosses some of the children had made. I also gave them a whistlestop tour of the events of Holy Week, and I'd like to share it with you too, because Holy Week is not just Palm Sunday, Good Friday, and Easter Day.

Palm Sunday, Jesus enters Jerusalem riding on a donkey and is greeted by cheering crowds waving palm branches and singing 'Hosanna, Blessed is he who comes in the name of the Lord.'

Holy Monday, Jesus cleanses the temple. He over turns the money changers' tables, and drives out the sellers of sacrificial animals. Not because what they were doing was wrong, it was required in Jewish law, no, because they were so intent on WHAT they did, they had forgotten WHO they were doing it for. 'My Father's house is a house of prayer,' said Jesus. Remember that, remember WHO you are here to worship and make that your focus.

Holy Tuesday, Jesus spends the day teaching. Teaching his disciples, teaching the people, spreading the news of the coming Kingdom of God, and trying to make them understand what was going to happen to him, and why.

Holy Wednesday, we don't know much about what Jesus did, but Holy Wednesday is also known as Spy Wednesday, the day Judas went to the Jewish leaders and offered to betray Jesus. Offered to hand over the Messiah for money.

Maundy Thursday, at supper with his friends, Jesus did three things. He took the role of a servant and washed the disciples' feet. He gave us the New Commandment, 'Love one another. As I have loved you, so you must love one another'. And he broke bread and shared wine, 'Do this in Remembrance of me'. At the service on Maundy Thursday, we will be remembering the first ever Last Supper – 'On the night before he died, which was this night'.

Good Friday, Jesus is crucified, he hands over the care of his mother to one of his disciples, he asks God to forgive the people, and then he breathes his last, 'It is finished'. He is taken down and placed in the tomb, and as far as his disciples, the Jewish leaders, the Roman authorities, and the people are concerned, that it is. It truly is finished.

Holy Saturday, Nothing happens. It can't. It is the Jewish Sabbath. In the church, it is a day of reflection and contemplation, a day spent in prayer.

Easter Day, Jesus Christ is Risen Today, Alleluia. The Greatest Day, the most important day in the year, the most important day in our history. Far from being finished, the story of Easter, the joy of the Glorious Resurrection, has only just begun for us and for the whole world.

This hasn't been the usual kind of Ramble, and my summing up of Holy Week may seem a little simplistic, but I hope that it will inspire you next week to think about what happened, to reflect on what Jesus did, not just during Holy Week but for the three years he spent with us, as one of us, and to maybe join us on Easter Day as we joyfully shout 'Jesus Christ is Risen Today. He is Risen Indeed. Alleluia', and to then go out into the world renewed, refreshed, and inspired to be like Jesus, and to do as he did – To love one another, as he loves us.

29th March 2024

Maybe I don't watch as much sport as I used to because I haven't seen it for years, but when I was growing up there seemed to be someone in the crowd at every Olympics, every World Cup final, in fact every major sporting event, holding a sign saying John 3: 16. Now I must admit that when I was 6 or 7 I probably couldn't have told you what it meant, in fact I probably thought it referred to one of the competitors, but of course now I know what passage in the bible it is highlighting.

'For God so loved the world that he gave his only begotten Son, so that all who believe in him will not perish but have ever lasting life'.

It will come as no surprise to most of you that such a well-known passage gets a lot of people, of faith and of none, very hot under the collar. They debate what it means by 'only begotten Son', they discuss what it means to have 'everlasting life', and they challenge each other's understanding of 'all who believe in him'. But on Good Friday, the day that Jesus died, what some people focus on is one simple word, gave. For God so loved the world that he GAVE his only begotten son.

The dictionary definition of gave, or in the present tense give, offers its use as both a noun and a verb, but they all suggest the handing over of something, or someone, to another for their use. To do with as they will. For those who like to debate, challenge, sometimes even ridicule others' faith and beliefs, it suggests that Jesus had no say in the matter, that he was handed over to be crucified with no chance of escape, no opportunity to change to course of events. But that suggests that God is not a God of love, is not a God of forgiveness, is not a God who wants the best for all his children.

Jesus came freely and willingly to teach and to preach the Good News of God's Kingdom, his kingdom. He came to save the world and to do so by showing the people how much God loved them, all of them equally. He came 'not to be served but to serve, and to give is life as a ransom for many' (Mark 10: 45). He came willingly, he came openly, he came in love, and he died that all might live.

All through his three years of ministry, Jesus prayed that the people would listen to him, prayed that the people would turn back to God, prayed that the people would accept all that God was offering them, but they didn't. And yet still, as he hung on the cross, being sneered at and jeered by the rulers and leaders, Jesus prayed not just for the people of Israel but for the whole world, not just for the people of that time but for the people of the future and of the past - 'Father, forgive them, for they do not know what they are doing' (Luke 23: 34).

On this Good Friday, and at our celebration of the Risen Christ on Easter Day, we need to ask ourselves – Do we know what we are doing? Do we accept Jesus' gift of eternal life? Do we accept his challenge to serve and not to be served? Do we, in our day to day lives, echo Jesus' words to his Father in heaven as he waited and prayed in the Garden of Gethsemane on the night before he died, 'Not my will but yours be done'.

'For God so loved the world that he gave his only begotten Son, so that all who believe in him will not perish but have ever lasting life'.

5th April 2024

(First Friday after Easter)

Many years ago, churches used to give out posters at the start of Holy Week, and sometimes even at the start of Lent, that had an image of Jesus and across the bottom the words 'He is Risen!'. The idea was that you put the poster in your window with the words folded up out of sight until Easter morning, when you unfolded it and declared the Easter Acclamation to the world, He is Risen!

I don't know why it stopped, but over a few years, the number of posters gradually reduced, and the idea just seemed to peter out. One reason may have been because there was often the same debate about how long you left the poster up as there is about how long Christmas decorations should hang around (excuse the pun). Did you take it down on Easter Monday? Did it stay up until Ascension Day or Pentecost, or in fact, should it stay up all year?

I've rambled before about my Holy Week reading, The Longest Week by Nick Page. I have read it every year for the last 10 years, and every year it is inspiring, challenging, and humbling. It offers a day-by-day account, indeed, on Good Friday, an almost hour by hour account, of the events leading up to the Greatest Day, leading up to the Resurrection. But perhaps the most inspiring, and humbling, passages don't come on one of the days of Holy Week, but in the final chapter, which the author has titled 'Aftershock'. What happened after the Resurrection, not just in the 40 days to Ascension, or the 50 days to Pentecost, but after that? How did the events of that first Easter Day 'change the world'!

Well, it inspired the men and women who had been hiding away in fear, after the Crucifixion, to burst out into the streets and proclaim 'He is Risen', and spread the Good News of the Kingdom of God. It has inspired millions of people over the past 2000 years to love one another, as Jesus loves us. It inspired Edith Cavell to treat wounded soldiers from both sides in the First World War; it inspired Corrie Ten Boom to help Jewish people escape the Holocaust in the Second World War; it inspires aid workers to go into places of conflict, places of natural disaster, places of danger, to help and to heal. It inspired William Wilberforce and Olaudah Equiano in their fight to abolish the slave trade. It inspired Martin Luther King, Oscar Romero, Maximillian Kolbe, Dietrich Bonhoeffer, and the 45 million Christians it is estimated died in the 20th Century for not just believing in God, Father, Son, and Holy Spirit, but for living their faith, for fighting against oppression, persecution, discrimination, and hatred.

We are all used to the posters at Christmas that say 'A pet is for life, not just for Christmas', well the events of Easter Day, the Greatest Day, are not just for one day, not just for 40 or 50 days, they are also for life, it's just up to us whether we put away the Easter Message as we put away our Christmas decorations, or whether we accept the challenge, the inspiration, the joy, of knowing the Risen Lord and taking Him with us everywhere we go, and seeing Him in everyone we meet. As Nick Page tells us in the last two lines of his book, 'That's the thing about the Longest Week. It never really did come to an end'.

Alleluia, he is Risen. He is Risen indeed, Alleluia.

19th April 2024

On the radio yesterday, the presenter was talking about what jobs are 'safe' from AI and bemoaning the fact that a Radio Presenter was not on the list. Apparently, there are already radio stations around the world where the voice is computer generated, and phone in sections can get very messy, and very funny, when strong accents cause confusion over what is being said. I have to admit that sometimes in this country I do wonder if what I am listening to is actually a real human being because what they say doesn't make much sense, but maybe that is just me!

So I decided to have a look online (where else) to see what jobs and professions are considered safe, and whether they matched the list I had in my own mind as to what I wouldn't want to see replaced by robots or AI Chat boxes (the bane of my life with banks and online shopping sites).

It turns out that scientists and programmers have realised, rather belatedly, that manual jobs, plumbers, electricians, heating engineers etc, will always need a human being. There are just too many variables, too many possibilities, that need to be assessed before anything can be done. Next on the list is hospitality and front-line retail. Yes, AI can generate menus, but it can't sauté, season, taste, and present food on the plate. Robots may be able to select, box, and dispatch from a warehouse, but they can't work on a shop floor with the 101 interactions that happen every day.

Next come those classed as the caring or tending professions. It includes teachers, Care Home workers, nurses, surgeons, carers in the community, and thankfully for me, priests and all religious activities. People who need to be able to see beyond a smile and an 'I'm fine', people who need to be able to hold someone's hand, to be able to stitch a wound or put a plaster on, while also restoring lost confidence and maybe healing a broken heart.

AI can do amazing things, but in all the hype and all the doomsday predictions, it is good to be reminded that there are some things AI can't do. It can't replicate empathy, compassion, or instinct. It can read an angry, sad, or happy face, but it can't see the pain behind a smile, the fear behind a frown, the forced gaiety hiding anxiety and worry.

Whether you are excited or nervous about the AI revolution, it has provided us with the chance to better understand, and celebrate, what makes us human, what makes us unique, special, blessed, and also to value the people who make our lives better and who provide us with the services we rely on.

Human beings are, for the most part, social beings, community based, supported and encouraged by fellowship and interaction with others, so the next time you have to call a plumber, pop to the shop, or need to see the nurse, greet them with a smile, and thank God that they are there, because AI can't replace them, and we need them.

26th April 2024

Did you watch the latest in the Pilgrimage Series on BBC2, when seven celebrities took to the highways and byways of North Wales in the footsteps of the Celtic Saints? I have to admit I have recorded it but haven't watched it yet, but I will do, because although sometimes the participants annoy me, or frustrate me, I find it fascinating and, yes, often inspiring to watch them as they go through the highs and lows that a Pilgrimage will often take you on.

I have been fortunate to visit several of the major Pilgrimage sites in this country and in Europe. I have been to the Holy Land, to St Peter's in Rome, to Walsingham, to Canterbury, and of course, in our own Cathedral, we have the Shrine of St Richard, considered by some to be the third most important Shrine in the country after that of Thomas Becket in Canterbury and Our Lady in Walsingham. But what is it about a Pilgrimage that still inspires so many people today? Why do over 400,000 walk the Camino de Santiago every year, beginning in France, or Portugal, or even Canterbury, and ending at the Church of Santiago de Compostela in Northern Spain?

The thing about a Pilgrimage is that the destination is not always the most important aspect. Pilgrimages begin the moment you step out of your front door, or switch off your mobile phone, even if you are going to be travelling most of the way by air, coach, or car. Pilgrimage is about the journey, and not just the physical, but the mental, emotional, and spiritual journey people go on when they leave the everyday behind. Pilgrimages can be hundreds of lines long, or a few miles around your local area, or you can even undertake a Pilgrimage without leaving home.

So, back to my question, what is it that inspires people to 'go on Pilgrimage'? Well, think back to Lockdown. For some people, the enforced slowdown, the enforced isolation, was a difficult time, but for others it was a time of renewal, a time of rejuvenation, and a time of discovery. People found a new appreciation for nature, a new understanding of the world around them, and took it as a chance to reflect on their lives and on their priorities. The same is often the case on a Pilgrimage. They are a chance to reassess our lives and to become better grounded in our faith, in our lives, and in our relationships. They are a chance to reflect on what is important, and what isn't, and to decide what, and how, you want your future to be.

It isn't always possible to go on an organised Pilgrimage, but just a couple of hours a week, with no emails, no mobile phones, no TV, in fact no distractions at all, can be an amazing experience, and can be life changing and life affirming. So, the next time you have some free time, don't try to fill it; take advantage of the opportunity to have a bit of a Pilgrimage at home, who knows what you may discover about yourself.

3rd May 2024

(Day after the Local Elections)

Did you vote on Thursday? Talking to the Presiding Officer at the Village Hall in Singleton, after I had cast my vote, she said it had been an understandably low turnout. Understandable because, unlike many other areas, we were just voting for the Crime Commissioner, and to be honest, I hadn't heard of most of the candidates and knew nothing about them. But I still voted, because I always remember what one of my teachers said, when as Sixth Formers I and my classmates were able to vote for the first time, 'If you don't vote, you can't moan. Even if your candidate doesn't win, you've had your say, you've taken part, and you've honoured the memory of those who fought and sometimes died to get you the right to vote!' Pretty serious stuff, but probably what we as 18-year-olds needed to hear. So as our A Level exams came to an end, we dutifully made our way to the Polling Station and put an X in our chosen box.

The next General Election in this country will probably be held in the autumn, and I don't know how many people will register to vote, or how many will actually vote, but it will be nowhere near as many as are currently taking part in the largest election in the world. In India, 969 million people are eligible to vote, that's roughly 1 in 8 of the world's population, and they take their right to vote very seriously. In the last election, 2 officials travelled for 2 days, by bus and on foot, to reach a remote region to ensure that the one eligible voter got to cast their vote! 2 days, I just hope the voter was in when they got there!

In the Acts of the Apostles, the members of the early church also got to decide who would represent them; they were called by Peter to choose who was to replace Judas in The Twelve. And just like modern elections, there were certain criteria that the candidates had to fulfil. They had to have been with Jesus since the beginning, from his baptism by John, right through to Ascension Day, the day he returned to Our Father in heaven. Now, the number of people involved was pretty small; we're told there were 120 people present, and there were just 2 candidates, Barsabbas and Matthias. And so, after a time of prayer, they cast lots for them, and the lot fell on Matthias'.

When I was a child and heard this story, I had an image of the disciples throwing dice (which is how the soldiers would have divided his clothes at the Crucifixion), or the two names being put in a hat and someone, probably Peter, drawing out the name of the chosen one. The latter is probably closer to what actually happened, and although we don't know who the 'Returning Officer' of the day was, it was probably Peter who drew out one of the small white stones usually used to settle disputes, decide land allocation, and on which the name of the newest Apostle was written.

So, did the disciples actually get to cast a vote as we would understand it? No, they trusted that the will of God would be revealed in the casting of lots? Which begs the question, can we dispense with all the palaver of an election and just put the names of the candidates in a bag and get the local Bishop or Archbishop to draw out the winning name? No. Although it is a tempting thought, and will be even more appealing as we get closer to the next election and are bombarded with Party Pollical Broadcasts, leaflets though our letterbox, and even occasionally candidates knocking on our door, God gave us, with the coming of the Holy Spirit at Pentecost, the privilege, and the responsibility, of using our free will fully and completely. We are in charge of our present and our future, and it is up to us how we use them.

Free will means we get to choose whether we follow the teaching of Jesus or not. We decide whether we treat others as we wish to be treated, or not. We can love one another as Jesus loved us, or not. We can focus entirely on ourselves, with no regard for the impact our words and actions have on others, or we can put the needs of others before our own wants. We can continue to ravage the earth to provide us with more food than we need, more clothes than we can possibly wear, and more technology than we can possibly use, or we can accept our role and responsibility as caretakers of God's earth and ensure a fair distribution of its resources now, and a better future for generations to come. The choice is ours.

10th May 2024

Yesterday (9th), the church around the world celebrated the Feast of the Ascension, one of the major Feast Days in the church calendar. It was an extra special day for me because I had the joy and the privilege of leading the Ascension Day service for Westbourne Deanery, of which The Valley Parish is a part. But although Ascension is one of the important Feast Days, one of the top five in fact, along with Christmas, Good Friday, Easter Day, and Pentecost, it is sometimes overlooked and not celebrated, at least not on the right day.

It is also sometimes misunderstood, as was demonstrated by a conversation I had a couple of weeks ago. While talking about Ascension, my fellow conversationalist, a wonderful regular customer in the shop called Joe, said, 'Ah, the end of the Long Goodbye'.

I didn't need to ask him to explain what he meant because I had heard Ascension called that before, and indeed had had some interesting debates about it. Jesus had spent the 40 days from his Resurrection meeting with his inner circle, the disciples, and being seen by, according to St Paul, over 500 of his followers. He had continued to teach and preach, and to try and get them to understand what his resurrection meant, and also that he would be leaving them soon. Joe saw the Ascension as the culmination of that time, when Jesus left earth to return to Our Father in heaven, and when he said his last goodbye, at the end of the long goodbye.

But to understand why Joe was both right and wrong in what he said, we need to think about what goodbye actually means. Goodbye is an abbreviation, a contraction, of the phrase 'God be with you', and not to be confused with Au Revoir, or Auf Wiedersehen, which mean 'till we meet again'. Now they are both, in their meaning, positive and uplifting phrases. To wish someone a safe journey in God be with you, or goodbye, or to affirm we want to see them again with au revoir, can be sad because we don't want them to go, but should also put a spring in their step because we are sending good wishes with them and can't wait for them to return.

Although at the Ascension Jesus was saying a human, earthbound, goodbye, not only was it not the end of his relationship with the disciples, or with us, 'I am with you always, to the end of the age' (Matthew 28: 20) it was also the time he promised the coming of a helper, a supporter, a strengthener, in the form of the Holy Spirit, which we will celebrate next weekend at Pentecost.

But as well as goodbye (God be with you) Jesus was also saying au revoir (till we meet again), because in John's gospel (14: 3) Jesus promises that his leaving is to go and prepare a place for us in heaven, and he will come and take us there, so that where he is we will be also.

So, back to my conversation with Joe. Although he was right in saying that Jesus said a final human goodbye to his disciples, it was not, is not, the end of our relationship with him. Jesus was in fact not saying God BE with you, but God IS with you, till we meet again.

24th May 2024

What's your breakfast routine like? At the Rectory, we have fallen into quite a good routine, I think. The first one up puts the kettle on and then goes to refill the bird feeders, by which time we are both up and between us we make the tea and coffee, put the toast on, and get the cereal ready. Because my sister and I like different things. I like coffee and cereal in the morning, usually, and she has tea and toast, usually. I say usually because sometimes we both have the same food wise, and sometimes we swap, I have toast, she has cereal. But what doesn't change is the beverage. I always have coffee, and she always has tea. It's our preference, our personal choice. Neither is right nor wrong.

I have rambled before on seeing things from another person's point of view, and on accepting that we don't all like the same things, or do things in the same way. But there is always the danger that personal choice becomes more than that. It is very easy to move from 'This is the way I like to do things' to 'This is the right way to do things', with the implied, or sometimes explicit, follow up 'what you do is wrong'. More often than not, the I'm right, you're wrong is actually a bit of a joke, a long running tease that involves not just individuals but groups of people, and sometimes whole counties. Think of the Cream Tea debate, is it jam then cream, the Cornish way, or cream then jam, the Devon way? The debate has been running for as long as there have been cream teas, and it is all done in good humour and has never, as far as I know, led to a war, a fight in the local tea shop, or a refusal to even sit down to eat with someone.

Sadly, the same cannot be said about religion. Not faith, but religion. Not who we believe in, but how we worship, what we do, and even when we do it. During my training, I spent time at two Evangelical churches, sometimes referred to as the happy clappy churches, and a friend spent time in two Anglo-Catholic churches, the bells and smells churches. We both had very similar experiences and came away determined to learn lessons in faith and worship from one, but equally determined not to fall into the ways of the other. One church was absolutely convinced that their way was the right way, the only way, to worship, while the other was open to different traditions, different viewpoints. Sadly, most of my training year experienced similar things in whichever church tradition they spent time in.

At the first church I visited, I was greeted with the words 'Oh good, you've come to see how real Christian's worship'. I was told that the crucifix I wore was wrong, and that a simple cross was right. I was told I had to raise my hands in worship during the modern worship songs, and use the modern version of the Lord's prayer. The minister led the service in everyday clothes because robes were wrong, and they didn't have a sermon; they had a talk. They had closed their minds to learning from anyone, and far from being inclusive as they claimed, they were incredibly exclusive. Do it our way or not at all.

The second church, where I spent 3 months on placement, could not have been more different. On my first Sunday, I was greeted warmly, was given a service sheet that explained not just what was to happen but what it meant, and invited to sit with a couple for worship, not left in isolation. Although their usual practise was not to robe, for 2 services a month, with the full agreement of the congregation, the clergy robed, to make me feel more at home, and they introduced a few traditional hymns into their music repertoire. I was invited to preach, to lead prayers, and organise a midweek youth service, in my tradition, in my preferred way of worship. Their attitude, expressed by the minister at the first service, was that I was not there to learn from them, but that we were all there to grow in faith, and grow in love, together. There was no right or wrong way to worship; what was important was that we worshipped, and we all had much to learn from each other.

I have used religion as an example of how easy it is to fall into the 'I'm right, you're wrong' trap over personal choice and taste, because it is where I have seen it at its most obvious, but the danger is there in everyday life. Maybe not over tea or coffee, toast or cereal, but every time someone disagrees with us it is easy to take it as a personal attack, to take it as an undermining of our way of doing things, when in reality it is their personal preference vs ours, and neither is right and neither is wrong, but it is nearly always a great opportunity to learn and to grow, in knowledge and understanding.

There is a well-known quote attributed to Voltaire which sums up what our attitude should be to those we disagree with - 'I may disapprove of what you say, but I will defend to the death your right to say it'. If only we all applied that to everything we did, from worship to politics, the world would be a better and more understanding place.

14th June 2024

Up to 10.30 am last Friday, this Ramble would probably have been about our holiday. About the beauty of Yorkshire and Warwickshire, about my ticking off two of my 'bucket list' places to visit, Fountains Abbey and Hardwick Hall, and about the people we had met. But then it all changed with a car accident. Now don't worry, this isn't going to be a 'pity me' Ramble, because although the car is a write off, everyone involved walked away. Yes, there are cuts and bruises, torn muscles and damaged ribs, but they will heal, the bruises will fade, and our strength and our confidence will return. No, this Ramble, as many of my Rambles have been, is about giving thanks, about being grateful, and about the inherent kindness, compassion, and goodness of humankind.

When the crash happened, half a dozen or so people stopped to help. Some made sure we were OK and safe. Others phoned the police and directed traffic, and gave us their phone numbers in case we needed witnesses. The police, fire brigade, and ambulance arrived quickly (thankfully, we didn't need the latter), and it seemed in no time the car had been moved off the road, the debris cleared, and the road reopened. And then when we had emptied the car, because we knew that once it was taken away, we wouldn't see it again, we sat and waited, apparently alone on a remote stretch of the A44.

But we were not alone, because as we waited for the recovery vehicle and taxi, about 20 people stopped to make sure we were OK, to make sure we had someone coming to collect us, and to ask if there was anything they could do. Car drivers, van drivers, and even a cyclist, interrupted their journey, took time out of their busy day, to offer help, to offer comfort. I have no doubt that many of them, if we'd asked, would have loaded us and our luggage into their car or van and taken us to a hotel or the nearest train station. I'm sure they would have lent us a mobile phone, or given us whatever food or water they had if we had asked. When the recovery vehicle arrived, the driver charged my mobile for me, made sure we had everything out of the car, and, despite instructions from head office, refused to leave until the taxi had arrived.

Once we were home, friends and neighbours provided us with food essentials, and some welcome treats to lift our spirits, a fellow priest took the service on Sunday, and the insurance company organised a hire car, and some physiotherapy for my sister. But even with the insurance company and legal team, when we were going through the questions about the accident, their compassion and care were evident.

It is so easy, watching the news, reading the papers, or scrolling through social media, to believe that people are selfish, inconsiderate, and only looking out for number one, but our experience last week showed that that is not the case. It didn't restore my faith in human nature, which has always been there, but it did strengthen it, and gave us even greater cause to be grateful and, yes, to count our blessings.

I don't know whether the people that helped us were Christian, I don't know if they were consciously or unconsciously following the golden rule of faith, treat others as you would wish to be treated, or if they thought about the story of the Good Samaritan, but they certainly showed some of the gifts of the Holy Spirit love, patience, gentleness, goodness, and above all kindness.

We are going to be bombarded over the next few weeks with politicians, journalists, possibly even friends and family, telling us what is wrong with the world and some of the individuals in it. We are going to be told of the failings of one party, while bigging up another. We are going to hear and see verbal and even physical attacks on individuals because of what they believe. But whatever the minority say or do, the majority of people are kind, considerate, compassionate, and loving. And for that, I will be forever grateful.

12th July 2024

Do you use all the different programs on the washing machine, or just one or two? Do you have apps on your phone that you rarely, if ever open? Technology is a wonderful thing, but sometimes it gives us more than we need, and more than we want. We've spent the last week getting to grips with a new car, well, new to us anyway. It is the same make and model as our old car, but when I said, in all innocence, to the dealer, 'that's good, because I know where everything is', he smiled and said, 'Oh, this will be a completely different driving experience'.

In the ten years between our old car and our new one being produced technology has moved on, and he's right, it is a different experience. Thankfully, it has a proper hand brake; I never did get on with the electric one in the hire car, but it doesn't have a CD player, an optional extra the first owner didn't include. Some of the new innovations are great, the digital display of speed, the built in sat nav, but others, like some of the programs on the washing machine, I'm not sure I will ever use, such as park assist or the speed limiter. I'm sure they are helpful, and maybe it's an age thing, but I don't want to lose the skill of parallel parking, or give up the responsibility of controlling, and being responsible for, my own speed.

It got me thinking about how much we have come to rely on technology in a very short space of time, and what we have lost in doing so. When I started work in the 1980's, very few people had mobile phones, and those that did carried around what looked like a brick! Now there are debates in schools and in parliament as to what age children should get their own phone. The office I worked in had 20 staff, and we shared 5 computers. By the time I left, everyone had their own desktop, and managers had laptops as well, enabling, encouraging, us to work from home in the evenings and at weekends. When I was growing up, not every home had a phone, and so you had to make sure you either had change or a phone card to go to the nearest phone box. Now, a lot of people don't carry any cash, and phone boxes have been turned into community resources, housing defibrillators or book exchanges, as we rely on our mobiles to not only make calls but also, in many cases, to pay for purchases as well.

But one of the biggest losses over the past few years of advancing technology has been the ability to engage with people, and our surroundings. How often do you get on a bus, sit in a waiting room, or even walk down the street, and find that everyone around you is absorbed by their phone or tablet? How often do you sit in a café or restaurant and realise there is no conversation happening around you because again people are engrossed in the news feed, or the latest WhatsApp message, or even watching the football, rather than talking to each other?

There are secondary schools that have now started giving lessons to their leavers on how to make a phone call, because they are so used to pretty much all communication being by text or email. They are giving lessons on how to start, and make, conversation, in idle chit chat, because that is how you engage, that is how to find out about people. I don't know if there still are, but there used to be 'mobile phone free' carriages on trains, encouraging people to not only talk to the people they are with, but also to look out the window, to see the beautiful world we live in. There are restaurants that offer a discount if everyone at the table locks their phone away in a cage for the entirety of the meal, encouraging conversation, engagement with each other, and with the staff.

Technology is a wonderful thing, but we can't, we mustn't, let it rob us of our individuality, our skills, our engagement with others, and with our world. Oh, and back to the car, yes, the sat nav is very useful on journeys to new places, or when there are unexpected road closures, but we still carry a road atlas, because the sat nav can't tell us what that amazing house we've just passed is, or what the monument on the hill is, or show us where we might want to take a detour to see a beautiful view, or visit an ancient ruin.

19th July 2024

Yesterday we went to Woolbeding Gardens. No idea why we have never been, after all, it is the closest National Trust property to us and it is open on a Thursday, but the fact is, we had never made it before. It is a beautiful garden, or rather gardens as they have embraced the idea of garden rooms and dedicated spaces, and is limited to 200 people a day, so as the guide said, 'how often can you visit a sold-out National Trust Garden and only bump into one or two people as you walk round'.

The picture at the top of this Ramble was taken at Woolbeding, at the amazing Glasshouse. As I walked out, my sister, still inside, saw my reflection in the entrance porch and told me to stop as she took the picture. The thing is though, the picture as you see it, is upside down! As we looked at it last night, my sister observed, 'It's a clearer image in the reflection'. Now there is a reason for that, the glass is slightly tinted, which I'm told sharpens the image. But it got me thinking about how often we see ourselves and our lives reflected back to us by the people we meet, the situations we find ourselves in, and even the culture we live in.

Sometimes it is a good thing; it sharpens our understanding of ourselves, and our lives, and brings clarity, just as the reflection of my image brought an extra clarity. I had a wonderful Spiritual Director for many years that I would go and see about every 2 months to talk through my ministry, my concerns and problems, and in fact everything about my life. More often than not, just telling him what was happening, how I was feeling, what my worries were, gave me a chance to see things more clearly; to get a clarity I hadn't been able to see as I mulled everything over in my own head. He didn't have to say anything, except maybe ask the odd question; he didn't try and give me the answers, he just let me talk and work things out for myself. The same is true with writing a journal. Just putting thoughts, worries, and issues down in words helps to make sense of what is happening, how we are feeling, and whilst we may not get all the answers, it does put things into perspective.

However, sometimes what we are doing when we talk with others, or when we look at the lives of other people apparently have, is not seeing a clearer reflection of our own lives, but in fact a distorted image. We end up comparing ourselves, and our lives, with what others have, or have done, or how they seem to be. We look at other people and see a perfect life, on the surface, or a successful career, on the surface, and we end up with an image of our lives that is twisted or misrepresented. We don't see what we are good at, or what blessings we have, because we don't think we are as good as the other person, or don't have what they have.

At last Sunday's service, I spoke about how people project themselves, how they distort their own image, especially on social media. How that perfect picture they posted on Facebook may have been taken 100 times before they found the right one. How that perfect holiday, with smiling faces and wonderful weather every day, would still have had the odd disagreement, the odd day of not-so-great weather. Their projected image, that they want the world to see, is not a true reflection of their life but is the life they wish they had, the life they think the world expects them to have. Photoshopped images of celebrities hide the fact that they too can have bad hair days, or bags under the eye's days.

289

The picture my sister took at Woolbeding is sharper in the reflection, but it doesn't change the reality, and I don't want it to. As I sit looking out over beautiful countryside, the life I see reflected back at me is one that I am content with, one that is blessed in so many ways. Yes, it has its ups and downs, yes, it has its problems, but it is my life, and it is one that I am truly thankful for.

26th July 2024

Road ahead closed, Diversion, I'm assuming that the regular increase in the number of these signs over the summer is not to deliberately upset everyone's holiday plans, but because (usually) it can be assumed there will be better weather and the work can be done more quickly, with hopefully less disruption.

Now, when I'm on a timetable, or on my way to an appointment, these signs can be (no, let's be honest, are) a pain and a nuisance. How much longer will my journey be? Should I stop and phone whoever I am supposed to be meeting to say I may be late, or should I give up entirely?

But when I'm not rushing somewhere, when I'm maybe just out for a drive, or coming back from somewhere, I find it very tempting to follow a random 'diversion' sign to see where it is a diversion to, having already wondered where it is a diversion from. I sometimes drive past the 'road ahead closed' sign just to see if it is my road that is closed, or, as so often seems to be the case, a little side road that very few people actually use. (of course, when I am in a hurry and drive past the sign, it seems that it is always the main road, my route, that is closed and I have to turn round!)

I have Rambled in the past on one of my favourite Bible passage, Proverbs 3: 5 – 6 (Trust in the Lord with all your heart and lean not on your own understanding; in all your ways acknowledge him, and he will make your paths straight.) and how God doesn't promise a flat path, or a pop hole free path, or a path with no road furniture. Well, he also doesn't promise a path that won't have the odd diversion or road ahead closed sign on it. Sometimes, when we believe we are following God's vision for us, when we think we are following God's path, we find ourselves stopped in our tracks by unexpected events, or diverted away from the way, the path, we think, we believe, we are called to follow.

The thing about the road ahead, closed or diversion signs in our lives, is that they don't necessarily mean we are going the wrong way, or are on the wrong path. It might be that we need to stop for a while where we are (road ahead closed, temporarily) to deepen our understanding, to maybe take a break, recharge our batteries, before we continue. Or it might be that we need to take a slight diversion to learn something, to see something, to experience something before we return to the original path, just as a diversion on the road can open up new views, new vistas, can let us see new places and maybe even meet new people before returning us back to our original route, a little bit further on.

292

Road ahead closed, diversion, can be a chance to see more, to encounter more, to grow more, and although they can be annoying and frustrating, they are also a wonderful opportunity to experience more of life, a wonderful opportunity to embrace more of the world, and of faith, and I pray that I, and you, will have the patience, and the courage, to embrace that opportunity fully.

2nd August 2024

(On Monday 29th July, seventeen-year-old Axel Radakubana entered a dance studio in Stockport and killed three children and injured ten others. In the subsequent court case, he was sentenced to a minimum of 52 years in prison, and a history of violence and extremist behaviour was revealed. However, none of this was known at the time of the attack, and I have decided to include this Ramble as I still believe we should not, we cannot, simply judge people on their race, religion or gender.)

My Ramble this week should have been about the Olympics, should have been celebrating the skill, dedication, and determination, of athletes from around the world, many of whom have overcome amazing odds to be representing their country. But the events in Stockport on Monday, and the headlines since, have overtaken the joy and excitement of gold medals, the disappointment of just missing that podium place.

Many of you will, I'm sure, remember the tragic events of 13th March 1996, when Thomas Hamilton entered Dunblane Primary School and killed 16 children and 1 teacher, and wounded 15 others, before killing himself. It was, and still remains, the worst mass killing of children in the UK. No one has ever gotten to the bottom of why it happened, what motivated Hamilton to attack the children, and we never will.

We may also never really know, or understand, what motivated Axel Muganwa Rudakubana to enter the dance school in Stockport and attack the children and adults inside. But it is the events after the attack, the headlines after the attack, that show how this country has changed in 28 years, and not for the better.

Following Dunblane, the headlines were of sympathy for the victims and their families, were of the bravery of the teachers who had shielded children, and were of the strength of the community in coming together to support each other. The headlines, just one day after the horrendous events on Monday morning, were of hate fuelled riots. A peaceful vigil, attended by thousands, was taken over by groups with a personal agenda, a political agenda, fuelled by misinformation, by fake news. The children who died, the children who witnessed what happened, the teacher who shielded them, the men who ran into the building to help, they have been driven off the front pages, they have been almost forgotten.

What is the difference between Thomas Hamilton and Axel Muganwa Rudakubana? The colour of their skin, and how recently their families came to this country. Thomas Hamilton, like Axel Muganwa Rudakubana, was a descendant of migrants, because 99% of us are. Yes, they may have come to this country 100, 500, or even 1000 years ago, but they were still migrants. Some, like the Vikings or Normans, were invaders, but this country has welcomed, over 100s of years, people escaping religious persecution, people escaping the Nazis in Germany and across Europe, people escaping the war in Ukraine. Most arrived with nothing, but they were welcomed, they were, are, supported, and helped.

The people provoking attacks on Mosques, attacking the same police officers who attended the dance school, even families who just happen to live in the local area, don't care about the victims, don't care about the added pain they are causing, don't care if what they are saying, what they are chanting, is true or not. They care about creating fear, hatred, and violence against people whose only 'crime' is to follow a different religion, to have a different skin colour.

But there is hope. The mother of one of the victims, who should have been able to focus on her grief on her family, has spoken out against the violence. The people of Stockport, still reeling from the events of Monday, have come together to repair broken windows and walls at the local Mosque. To clear the streets of burnt-out cars. They have rallied to support each other as the people of Dunblane did, as the people of Hungerford did in 1987. They have come together to repair the pain and hurt, the damage that can't be seen, and can barely be expressed.

My prayers, as we head into what is sadly expected to be a weekend of further violence, further riots, are for the victims, their families, those injured physically and mentally by what they saw and experienced, and for peace, understanding, and tolerance. We are justly proud of the freedoms we enjoy in this country. Freedom of speech, freedom of movement, freedom of religion, freedom of protest. But with those freedoms come a responsibility, a responsibility to use them well, to use them right, to use them for good and not for evil.

9th August 2024

What a difference a week makes.

Last weekend, the headlines were full of anger, hate, and acts of violence against anyone and everyone who got in the way of the rioting mobs. Shops were looted, wheelie bins set on fire, police officers assaulted, and in what is a huge no no in this country, police dogs also came under attack. The violence caused several countries around the world to issue travel warnings to their citizens, and even Elon Musk, for reasons known only to himself, weighed in with a declaration on Twitter (or X as we are now supposed to call it) that 'Civil War is inevitable'.

Well, Mr Musk, you were wrong. Yes, this week, thousands took to the streets again, up and down the country, but not to cause damage, not to spread hate, but to spread love, tolerance, and kindness. Far Right protesters in Brighton on Wednesday were outnumbered 100 to 1 by the people who came out to show support for their community and for their country. A community, a country, that includes people of all races and religions. The same happened up and down the country. Where there had been violence, communities came together to clear up the mess. Where there had been injuries, people rallied to support those injured. Where shops had

298

been boarded up in fear, the boards were covered in graffiti announcing Love will Win.

Yes, there are still issues, genuine concerns, with some towns and cities overwhelmed by the number of refugees and immigrants, but what has been shown over the last week is that violence, hatred, is not the answer, and that those refugees, those immigrants, are not responsible for every problem, for every issue, we face. The Far Right, and Elon Musk, hoped to use a shocking, sad, and emotionally charged event, the stabbings in Southport, for their own ends. They wanted to hijack the grief of the families, the shock of a community, for their own ends. But after the first riot, after they hijacked the peaceful vigil after the stabbings, the writing was on the wall. The people of Stockport, still reeling from the events of the day before, came out in force to clear up the mess. They came out in force to repair the damage done to the Mosque, to clean up the streets. They came out in force to show that they, we, will not be intimidated.

I don't know how many of the people who took to the streets of Brighton, Hastings, and London, this week to advocate peace, to advocate love, to show us hope, were Christian. I don't know how many of them would know the prayer of St

Francis of Assisi, but it is a prayer that was answered in the spreading of love, hope, and peace.

Lord, make me an instrument of Your peace;
Where there is hatred, let me sow love;
Where there is injury, pardon; Where there is doubt, faith;
Where there is despair, hope; Where there is darkness,
light;
And where there is sadness, joy.

O Divine Master,
Grant that I may not so much seek to be consoled as to
console;
To be understood, as to understand;
To be loved, as to love;
For it is in giving that we receive, it is in pardoning that we
are pardoned,
And it is in dying that we are born to Eternal Life.
Amen.

16th August 2024

I'm sure many of you have been waiting on tenterhooks this week to see if your children or grandchildren got the A level results they needed or wanted. It has been, for many, a stressful time, and probably not helped by the intense media coverage. Now I have to admit that I barely remember getting my A Level results 40 odd years ago. Maybe because I wasn't planning on going to university, maybe because we had to wait for them to come in the post, or maybe because without social media, there wasn't the pressure to share results instantly.

However, I do remember waiting, not very patiently, for the results of my BAP residential in 2012. BAP stands for Bishops' Advisory Panel, and they are responsible for saying yes or no to whether someone should be recommended for training to the Priesthood. The system has changed now, but in 2012, a BAP involved a 3-day residential in Ely, which included giving a presentation, undergoing 3 very intensive interviews, and engaging in group sessions. The result of a BAP was, as with my exam results, sent by post, but the Diocesan Director of Ordinands (DDO) was sent the details in advance and phoned each candidate to tell them personally. The call was due on a Friday, between 6 pm and

9 pm, and so the night before, although I was nervous and a little distracted, I had settled down in front of the TV when the phone rang at 9.30 pm. It was the DDO to tell me that the BAP had said yes. As with many of the A Level students we have seen on TV this week, I was excited and also a little overwhelmed. I had been working towards that day for almost 2 years, and to be told that I had been accepted was genuinely a life changing moment.

But along with the congratulations, and the practical matter of what happened next, the DDO had some sage advice. Don't forget, he said, others didn't get the result they wanted. Be careful and be considerate of others when you share the news. It was good advice, because only a few months earlier, a friend from my then church had also attended a BAP and they had not been recommended for training. It was a difficult conversation to have with them, but one I made sure I had before I told the result to anyone outside of the family, because for both of us, in different ways, the result of our BAP had been life changing.

With all of the media attention on exam results at the moment, it is almost impossible for those who didn't get the grades they needed to avoid the excitement and celebrations of those who did. It is almost impossible for those who did get the grades to show the consideration and compassion they want to those who didn't.

We also need to be aware of those around us whose lives have not turned out the way they hoped. Who didn't get the opportunities or have the advantages, many of us did. We need to be aware of how our lives look to them. How we act around them. We need to make sure we follow the words of the prophet Jeremiah "Thus says the Lord, Let not a wise man boast of his wisdom, and let not the mighty man boast of his might, let not a rich man boast of his riches." (Jeremiah 9:23).

We need to remember to be thankful without boasting, and to share what we have with a generous and compassionate heart, because we have so much more than so many people, in this country and around the world, and we must show our gratitude for all we have in who we are, how we are, and how much of our blessings we share.

30th August 2024

I'm sure many of you are Antiques Roadshow fans, or used to watch things like Fake or Fortune, and like me are often left speechless by the financial value placed on some items. You may also, again like me, have been equally surprised by the fact that some items that I would have expected to be worth a lot of money are valued at only a few hundred pounds. Of course, a painting by Picasso, a vase by Lalique, or a first edition by Conan-Doyle carries a large price tag because of their rarity. Other items have an increased value because of who owned them, used them, or wore them. A pair of Victorian bloomers might make a couple of hundred pounds, but add in the fact that they were worn by Queen Victoria, and you can add a couple of noughts to the price.

But what I really love about shows like the Antiques Roadshow is the reaction of the people. Some, I'm sure, already knew the value of their item, judging by their reaction, but for most it comes as a complete shock. The vase they had been using as an umbrella stand, the chunky ornament they had as a door stop, the small table they had in their hallway, suddenly have a possibly life changing value. But for many of them, there is no intention of selling. Yes, the old vase that was just an umbrella stand will now take pride of place in their sitting room, but it was a gift to an ancestor from a grateful employer, the chunky ornament was a wedding present to their parents, and the hall table came from their grandmother. The value they place on the item isn't financial but personal, and comes with an emotional attachment, an emotional value, that no amount of money can ever match.

We often see that same emotional attachment in St Olav's bookshop. One of the joys of our second-hand section is when someone excitedly comes up to the counter with an old, maybe slightly worn, book, and they tell us that they had the book as a child, or it was a gift for their confirmation, but they lost it, or it got damaged. They are so excited to be able to replace it, about being able to relive, remember, those 'priceless' moments.

Of course, everything we own has a price tag. It may be worth a few pounds, it may be worth a few thousand pounds, it may be worth a lot more, but what is its real value to us? A book from our second-hand section may only cost £1, but to the new owner, reliving, remembering, it is almost priceless. To the owner of their grandmother's hall table, the value is in the memories, the value is in the relationship they had with her, and that is also priceless.

Probably the most famous quote in the bible comes from John's Gospel. 'For God so loved the world that he gave his one and only Son, that whoever believes in him shall not perish but have eternal life.' (3:16). It is one of many quotes that remind us not only of God's love, but also our value to him. We are priceless to God. Later in the New Testament, in the first letter of John, he reaffirms that idea "See what great love the Father has lavished on us, that we should be called children of God! And that is what we are!" (1 John 3:1). It doesn't matter how much we earn, how much we are worth in the eyes of the world. It doesn't matter if we live in a mansion or a slum, it doesn't matter if our walls are adorned with Old Masters or prints downloaded from the internet. All that matters is that we are all unique and priceless in the eyes and the heart of God. If only the whole world saw every human being in the same way, what a wonderful, priceless world it would be.

6th September 2024

As regular readers of my Rambles will know, I love it when there is livestock in the field behind the Rectory, especially when they are on the hill. I love sitting over my morning coffee and watching them as they make their way across the field, watching as they interact with each other. I am especially pleased at the moment because we have sheep, admittedly very noisy sheep, but sheep that are fascinating to watch. From happily grazing, they will all, suddenly, start to head off left to Charlton, or right over to the tree line that runs up the hill. Now the latter, especially today, is probably because they are trying to get some shelter from the rain, but whatever the reason, the whole flock seems to suddenly get up and move as one.

Now you will probably all have heard, if not used, the saying 'follow like sheep'. It is a disapproving, critical saying, suggesting people follow trends, follow orders, follow leaders, without thinking for themselves. It is a saying that has its roots in the Middle East, where sheep are not herded as they are in this country, from the back of the flock, but lead by the shepherd from the front. It is a saying that is also sometimes problematic for Christians, because Jesus frequently calls the people of Israel sheep, Lost sheep without a shepherd (Matthew 9: 36) is just one example. It is a saying that is often also used as a criticism of Christians, suggesting that those who follow the teaching of Jesus, follow the commandments of God, do so without thinking about, reflecting on, or even understanding, what they are doing, or why they do it.

But the analogy of sheep and a shepherd, and a Good Shepherd at that, used in the Bible is not one referring to the blind following of doctrine, the simple 'follow the leader', that we seem to see with the sheep in the field. When Jesus refers to the people of Israel as sheep without a shepherd, he is referring to the fact that they had teachers, they had Rabbis, they had leaders, who expected the people to follow them blindly. They didn't have compassion for them; they didn't care about their lives, about their souls. They expected the people to do what they were told; they expected them to follow like sheep.

Jesus, however, calls himself the Good Shepherd. The shepherd who knows his sheep, his people, and his people know him. The shepherd who calls his sheep, his people, and invites them to follow him, trusting that he will bring them nourishment, will care for them, and will bring them safely to where they are going. The Good Shepherd is the one who cares about the lost sheep, who will look for them and bring them back to the flock. But unlike the shepherd who will hoist a lost sheep on his shoulders and carry it back, Jesus, the Good Shepherd, doesn't force us back into the fold, doesn't expect us to blindly follow him. He calls us by name and hopes, prays, we will respond, will answer him, and will return to him. He doesn't want us to unquestioningly follow; he doesn't want us to be like the sheep in the field; he wants us to use the God given gift of free will to choose to follow. And when we do, he will be The Good Shepherd. He will care for us and about us. He will walk with us, gently leading us, guiding us, encouraging us, because he knows us, has called us by name, and we are his. We just have to choose whether we answer or not.

13th September 2024

I spent yesterday morning watching as some of the trees in the Rectory garden were cut back (technical term is, I understand, 'crowning'). It was fascinating to watch, and a real eye opener in many ways. I hadn't realised that the tree was so thick that a man in a high vis suit could stand on one of the branches and I wouldn't be able to see him! It is also hard to appreciate quite how big the tree is until you compare it to the man standing in it!

As well as cutting back on height, they have also raised the canopy, letting more light get to the ground below its branches. We can't wait to see what emerges next spring, seeds and even potentially bulbs, that have lain dormant for years, waiting for the light and the heat to reach the ground. They also cut away some of the dead wood, reducing the weight on some of the branches and allowing them to spring back to where they want to be, where they should be.

It got me thinking about the amount of dead wood we carry around in our lives. The extra weight (not the physical kind) that we have to cope with every day. We all have dead wood. We all have past hurts, past pains, past issues, even past insults, that we just don't seem to be able to shake off. They affect how we think, feel, behave, and how we react to other people and to new situations. They affect how we think about ourselves, they affect our relationship with others, and our relationship with God, because they can make us blind to all the opportunities, all the joys, and all the possibilities that are waiting to be explored, grasped, and enjoyed.

In John's Gospel (ch 15, vs 1 – 2), on the night before he died, Jesus told his disciples that he was the true vine, and God the vine-grower, and that God removes every branch that bears no fruit, and prunes those that do, so that they will bear more fruit. We need to do the same. When we carry around our deadwood, when we let thoughts, feeling, attitudes, weigh us down, we are cutting ourselves off from the light, stopping us from enjoying other parts of our lives that are laying dormant, waiting for us to acknowledge them, waiting for us to free them so that they, we, can blossom, grow, and bear more fruit.

I know it can be hard to forget the past, especially if that past caused us pain, but just as with the trees in the Rectory, and the vine that God prunes, if we can, if we can throw away all the deadwood we carry, we will not only feel lighter, but we will be able to enjoy all that we have now, we will be able to look to the future, and we will be open to new experiences, new relationships, and a new and fulfilling life, in all its fullness.

18th October 2024

Last week, my sister and I had a week of doing nothing! Well, not entirely a week of doing nothing, we got up, we breakfasted, we had lunch, dinner, and went to the evening entertainment the hotel laid on. In between the showers, some of them monsoon like, we strolled around the grounds of the hotel, and visited the Roman Mosaic rediscovered 200 years ago. But we didn't go anywhere. We didn't do our usual round of National Trust properties, local gardens, and places of interest. The hotel we were staying at is based around a Tudor Manor, and so we spent four days ensconced in the library of the old house and just read.

The past few months have been challenging and difficult for both of us in different ways, and this holiday, booked many months ago, came at just the right time, and gave us just what we needed – peace, quiet, tranquillity, and the chance to recharge our batteries. But would we have felt differently about what we did, about what we should be doing, if the weather had been better. If each morning we had woken up to bright sunshine rather than heavy showers, would we have felt we HAD to go out of the hotel. Would the worldly expectation that we have to be busy, have to be up and at 'em all the time, have overridden our need for rest and relaxation.

I don't suppose many of our fellow guests opened their curtains in the morning and smiled as they said, 'It's raining again', but I did. I don't suppose many of our fellow library occupants would have said they were glad to be sitting there, watching the rain lash the windows, and partly flood the putting green, but I was. The rain gave us the chance to say no, we're not going to go out, we're not going to visit crowded historic houses, we're just going to sit and be.

It is so easy to feel guilty if we take time out, if we ignore the demands of emails, phone calls, the washing up in the sink, the hoover in the understairs cupboard, but we shouldn't, because we have a wonderful guide, a wonderful champion, of the need to take time out, to withdraw from the world and all its demands, and that champion is Jesus. There are many examples in the Gospels of Jesus 'withdrawing from the crowds', sometimes alone, sometimes taking some or all of his disciples with him. Times when he went up a mountain, or across the Sea of Galilee, or simply withdrew to a quiet place, to pray, to recharge, to rest.

Jesus, fully human and fully divine, understood the need for us to retreat sometimes from the world's demands. He came to serve, to heal, and to teach, but even he, the Son of God, needed to take time away from the crowds, to be with God, to pray, to be restored. He understood that sometimes we see so much around us that needs doing, fixing, so many people that need our help, need our time, that it is difficult for us to turn away, difficult for us to shut the door. He saw it in his own disciples and so he took them to quiet places, places they could eat, rest, and sleep. Not for days on end, usually only for an hour or two, but just enough time for them to relax and refresh.

So the next time you take time out, the next time you decide to switch off the phone, the computer, the list of jobs that need doing around the house, because you can't face them, remember that so did Jesus. He didn't do it because he didn't care, he didn't do it because he was lazy, he did it because he knew that in order to care for others, we have to care for ourselves. He did it because he knew that he couldn't love others if he didn't love himself, and that meant taking care of himself, his disciples, and his followers. Attending to his needs as much as he attended to the needs of others.

The next time it rains on a day you planned to spend in the garden, or the next time the internet goes down when you planned to spend the day answering emails, take it as a chance to recharge and renew, a chance to be like Jesus and withdraw for a few hours from the demands of the world and look to yourself and your needs. If you do, you will come out the other side refreshed, refocused, and better equipped to face all that the world can throw at you.

25th October 2024

Yesterday I was invited, with other adults, to a guided tour of Singleton Village by the pupils of Beech Class from Singleton School. It was a fascinating walk around the village because not only did we get to see places and events through the eyes of the children, but we also found out about what they were most interested in, by what they focused on. Although for Health and Safety reasons each tour followed the same route, and at times the small groups did join together, the children had done their own research, produced their own maps, and written their own scripts. For one group, history was important, the dates and ages of the buildings. For another, it was pointing out where friends lived. For a third, it was the play area on the Glebe Field. I didn't get to over hear the other groups, but I'm sure their tours also revealed as much about the children as they did about the Village.

When someone is passionate about a subject, there is something almost mesmerising about it. It could be a speaker at the WI, a member of a Book Club, or a room guide at a National Trust property. I may not share their passion for a particular hobby, a recently read book, or a particular period of history, but I can appreciate their zeal for the subject, especially if they are open to questions, open to being challenged as to what they find so fascinating, so engaging, about their subject, about their passion, and if they are willing to listen to another's point of view, to learn from someone else's knowledge. The children on our tours were not only open to questions from the adults, but they were also keen to ask us questions, to find out what we knew about the places we visited, about the history of the Village, and in my case, the history of the church.

But what if people are not willing to listen to others, not willing to see others' point of view? Well, at its simplest level, they are cutting themselves off from some fascinating conversation, and the chance to maybe learn a little more about their favourite subject. At a more serious level, it can lead to arguments, to fractures within a group or a family, and taken to extremes, it can lead to wars and conflicts.

I have no doubt that when the children were doing the research for their tours and deciding on what buildings, places, and events to focus on, they had a few disagreements. I'm sure not everything each child wanted to say or do was incorporated in their particular tour. They had to compromise on what they included and what they left out, maybe because of time, maybe because of the practicality of visiting places slightly off the beaten track. I'm sure some of the children had to accept that what they were interested in wasn't right for the day. But I am also sure that the teaching they have received on the value of each person, on the importance of listening to others, meant that they were heard by their fellow tour guides. Meant that they were listened too, appreciated, and valued.

We don't all share the same passions, we don't all share the same religious and political views, and we don't all agree all the time. But when we do disagree, when we find our voice to be the only one speaking from a particular viewpoint, we need to learn from the children not just of Singleton School but West Dean as well, and we need to listen to each other, value each other, and maybe agree to disagree, but with love and with understanding, not digging our heels in, not burying our heads in the sand, not ignoring the other or declaring them wrong. Appreciating the value to each person, accepting we each have our view point, our own passions, our own interests, but having a commitment to work together for the good of all, for the common good - that is the way schools, churches, communities, families can flourish, grow, and become stronger.

8th November 2024

Go in peace, to love and serve the Lord.

These are the last words I say to the congregation every Sunday, after offering the blessing. The same words are said in churches across this country, and across the world, at the end of every Christian service of Holy Communion. They are said in a multitude of languages, in a multitude of places. But even as I say them, I know that we are blessed in this country that we can leave church and go out into what is predominantly a peaceful country. The same cannot be said of the people leaving churches, mosques, synagogues, or meeting houses in Ukraine, Palestine, Israel, Lebanon, and the 40 or so other countries where wars or conflicts rage around the world.

As we approach Remembrance Sunday, we can give thanks for the fact that the number of names added to the National Memorial, recording the members of the Armed Forces killed on active duty, gets smaller and smaller each year, with just one name added in 2023, but again, we cannot help but see the news headlines telling us of both military personnel and civilians who are being killed every day in countries not that far away.

With so much conflict going on around the world, with so much hatred, is it right or wrong that this weekend we come together for Remembrance Sunday? It is noticeable, walking around Chichester, how few poppies there are around this year, when I can remember that it wasn't that long ago that everyone wore a poppy, or had a poppy logo on their car. In the week leading up to Remembrance, cadets and old soldiers would be out on the streets, poppy boxes and collecting tins in hand. This year, a few shops have boxes; there is a stand outside the Assembly Rooms, and we have boxes in all our churches, but they are getting fewer and fewer each year.

Is it the number of ongoing conflicts that is making people turn away from Remembrance, or is it the fact that we in this country haven't seen or felt the effects of war first hand for a long time? Is it because we see Remembrance as being about the First and Second World Wars, and there are few people alive today who can tell us first-hand what those conflicts were like, that Remembrance is low on so many people's agendas? Or is it that Remembrance is seen as unimportant, almost irrelevant, in our 21st Century world

Remembrance isn't just about the two major conflicts of the 20th Century, nor is it a glorification of war. Yes, Remembrance Sunday is a time to remember all those who have died in all wars and conflicts, both armed forces and civilians, but it is also a time to reflect and pray for those still affected by war. It is a time to look back and see what lessons we can learn from the past, and pray we can put those lessons into practice. Winston Churchill said, 'Those who cannot learn from history are doomed to repeat it.' Remembrance Sunday reminds us of the price that has been, and is still, being paid by people who fight to defend their homeland, who fight for freedom from oppression, who fight for what we take for granted, free speech, freedom of worship, freedom of movement, freedom to vote.

This Remembrance Sunday, at West Dean, after saying the words at the top of this Ramble, we will begin our first Act of Remembrance, when we will remember all those from the Valley Parish who gave their lives for our freedoms. In the afternoon, at 3 pm, we will gather at the War Memorial in Singleton for another simple Act of Remembrance, when again we will remember those who have died, and those whose lives have been affected by war. At the beginning of each Act of Remembrance, these words will be said, *"What*

does the Lord require of you but to do justice, love kindness,
and to walk humbly with your God. "

To do justice and love kindness - and to go in peace – and to
commit ourselves to learning from the past, and the present,
and praying that our future will be one of peace and justice
for all - That is what the people we remember on Sunday
would ask of us.

15th November 2024

What do you think of when you look at the picture above? A football match, a Taylor Swift concert? No, the pictures show some of the 15000 people who turned up the day after the devastating floods in the Valencia region of Spain, with one purpose - to help. They came from far and wide, not just from Spain but from across Europe. People took time off work; students took time out of universities. There were families, individuals, and community groups. Farm workers who had driven their tractors for miles with one purpose and one purpose only – to answer the question 'when I needed a neighbour, where were you there?' with a resounding Yes.

The Parable of the Good Samaritan in the Bible is told in response to the simple question – Who is my neighbour? (Luke 10: 29 – 37). For the people who left the stadium armed with brooms, mops, buckets, even simple pieces of wood, the answer to the question 'who is my neighbour' is obvious – everyone. No matter what nationality, what skin colour, no matter how many miles away someone lives, they are our neighbours, and we all have a duty, a call, to help whenever and however we can.

There is obviously a lot of anger and grief in Spain right now. Anger at the government, anger at the local authorities, and grief at the loss of life, the loss of homes, businesses, and even whole communities, but there is also hope, and a commitment to work together to rebuild broken lives, restore homes, and reestablish communities. That hope comes from the outpouring of support, the outpouring of love, that we see in the picture above, and have seen day after day on our TV screens and in our newspapers. As the days go by, and the mud is slowly cleared from the streets, the people are also beginning to laugh again, beginning to sing again, beginning to live again. They have faith, they have hope, they have love, and the greatest of these is love.

Many of the people who have been in Valencia since the floods first hit are now preparing to move to Malaga, if they are needed. They have put their lives on hold to put the needs of others first. One man said 'I have a home to go back to. I have a job to go back to. I had to come and do what I could.'

It is so easy when faced with events on TV or social media for us to feel helpless, to feel frustrated, to feel there is nothing we can do, and maybe we can't help with the clear up after the floods, maybe we can't put our arms round the people whose lives have been devasted by wars, but we can pray for them and we can commit to doing what we can, when we can, the next time our neighbour, in the next house, the next street, the next country, the next continent, needs us.

When I needed a neighbour, were you there? Let us pray that the next time someone needs us, individually or as a community, our answer will be the same as the people who travelled to Valencia, let our answer be Yes.

13th December 2024

What are you most looking forward to at Christmas? What is your expectation, anticipation?

We had a lovely mother and son come into the shop on Wednesday, looking for only one thing – The Baby Jesus. Apparently, every shop they had gone into, every stall at the Christmas Market they had stopped at, the little boy's first question was 'Where's the Baby Jesus?'. He must have been about 3, and he got very excited as his Mum showed him all of our Nativity Sets, all of the cards that have images of the Nativity, and then found a book for him with a picture of Jesus, in the manger, on the front. He reluctantly handed the book over to me so I could scan it through the till, and then held it very close when I gave it back.

It got me thinking about how what we anticipate, what we get excited about, as Christmas approaches, changes over time, but should it?

The little boy in the shop was overwhelmed by all the lights and the music. He was very excited about all the things going on around him, but he had a wonderfully simple expectation of Christmas, the Baby Jesus. As he grows, the anticipation of what Christmas morning will bring will change. If he is anything like me, as a child, the most exciting thing about

Christmas was waking up really early (usually about 4 am!), waking my sister, and rushing into our parents' bedroom with the pillow case they had put at the foot of the bed and excitedly pulling out a few presents, and then delving deep to find the obligatory satsuma and nuts.

As we get even older, our anticipation, our excitement, can be about the presents, have we got what we wanted, have we got others what they wanted. It can be about visiting family and friends, about having family and friends visit us. Christmas parties, be they with friends or work colleagues, fill our diaries. Shopping, cooking, writing cards, wrapping presents, all have to be fitted in as we get closer and closer to the big day.

But what if we stopped for a few minutes and thought about the little boy and his one question - Where's the Baby Jesus? Where's the Baby Jesus in all our Christmas madness? Where's the Baby Jesus in all our rushing around? Where's the awe and wonder, where's the hope filled anticipation of the coming of the Son of God, the Light of the World?

I hope and pray that as that little boy grows up, as the world he knows gets bigger, as his Christmas experiences change, he will continue to have that one question as the heart of all he does, Where's the Baby Jesus? It is a question we all need to stop and ask ourselves as we approach Christ's Mass, where is the Baby Jesus in our lives?

28th December 2024

I'm sometimes asked where I get the inspiration for my Rambles from – some come from local or national events, some come from conversations in the Parish or in the shop, but today's inspiration was missing parsnips!

Let me explain. We thought we were ahead of the Christmas game. We'd done our last shop a few days before the Big Day, we'd got all the cards delivered, presents wrapped, and even remembered to get the gammon out of the freezer. But while I was enjoying the wonderful Carols and Crib on Christmas Eve, my sister, when she got home from work, started preparing the vegetables and realised we hadn't bought any parsnips. Now it wasn't a major, or even a minor, issue. We had plenty of other veg, and to be honest, our plates were overflowing anyway, so although it was a little annoying, it didn't affect our enjoyment of Christmas lunch, or Christmas Day. It did, however, get me thinking about how often we focus on what we don't have, rather than what we do.

Now I have rambled before on counting our blessings, on focusing on the positive, not the negative, and so you may be rolling your eyes and thinking 'here she goes again,' and I understand that for some, this Christmas was difficult. You may have spent your first Christmas without a loved one because they are no longer with us. It may have been the first Christmas without your children around because they now live hundreds or thousands of miles away. It may have been the first Christmas you spent alone, and I'm not in any way attempting to lessen the feelings of pain or grief. They are real, they are true, they are important feelings, and they are feelings that we all experience at some time, and often they are felt more keenly at Christmas when we are bombarded with images of happy families, of perfect Christmas, on TV and social media.

But even in our times of sadness, of grief, we can find the blessings. We cry because we loved, and were loved, and that love never ends. Simple acts remind us of how much we are loved, appreciated, and remind us of our blessings. It may be continuing a family Christmas tradition, as we do at the Rectory, reminding us of our parents. It may be in the Christmas card from a childhood friend. It may be the neighbour who knocks on the door on Christmas Day to wish us Happy Christmas, or the unexpected phone call from the other side of the world.

In the week before Christmas, we sat down to watch a classic sit com, The Good Life Christmas Special - when Margot's

Christmas wasn't delivered. As far as she was concerned, Christmas was cancelled, Christmas was a disaster, but then Tom and Barbara turned up and gave her, and Jerry, the best Christmas they had ever had. A simple Christmas, a Christmas without expensive presents, without the perfect food, the perfect decorations. A Christmas that contained one thing, and one thing only, love.

I hope you had a blessed and peace filled Christmas, a Christmas where you knew you were surrounded by love, from near and far, from earth and from heaven, and I pray for a 2025 that will give you new blessings, new hope, new peace.

3rd January 2025

Last night, my sister and I sat down to watch an amazing program on TV – 2024 – A year from space. The program used images from the 7000 satellites currently circling our planet to look back at the events of 2024 from a different perspective. It showed images of the scars humankind has made from wars, mining, and the damming of rivers, but also the beauty and diversity of the planet we call home. It showed a lunar eclipse as seen from the International Space Station, and the tell-tale signs that an Emperor Penguin colony had survived the harsh Antarctic winter. The Winter Festival in China, a whole village made entirely from snow and ice, lit up the night sky, and the coming of spring saw fields burst into colour. It also showed the effects of natural disasters, hurricanes, typhoons, and flooding, and told how satellite images were used to give advance warning and save lives.

Throughout the program, the voices of astronauts who had been on the International Space Station, and engineers who monitor the images from the satellites, gave a context to what we were seeing. One of the most poignant was at the end of the program when one of the astronauts commented, and hoped, that if everyone in the world could see what he had seen – the beauty, the diversity, and the fragility, of our planet, then everyone would want to save it, and there would be an end to wars and destruction.

Listening to him reminded me of one of my favourite songs – From a distance.

In the lyrics of the song, which has been recorded by Bette Midler and Cliff Richard, amongst others, we are reminded that from a distance, looking down on our beautiful planet, we all have enough. From a distance, there is harmony. From a distance, there is hope, and there is peace.

The song also contains the line, God is watching us. For some people, God is watching us from a distance. For them, he is a God who set us on this planet, gave us free will, and then left us to it. He is remote, far off, detached. But we have just celebrated the act that shows us that God is very much with us, here, on earth. In the birth of his Son, fully human as well as fully divine, we have the proof, if proof were needed, that God has not 'left us to it'. He cares about us, and on Good Friday we are reminded just how much, His Son was prepared to show just how great God's love is – to lay down his life for his friends, for us. And then on Easter Sunday, we will celebrate not only the outpouring of God's love, but the assurance of God's forgiveness and the promise of eternal life.

As we enter 2025, each of us with our own hopes, fears, dreams, and doubts, we can choose to look at events that happen on the other side of the world, or in the next street, from a distance. We can choose to step back and decide that we are too small, too insignificant, too unimportant, to make a difference, or we can take to our hearts the words of the Dalai Lama, 'if you think you are too small to make a difference, try sleeping with a mosquito'. We can all make a difference; we can all do small things to promote peace, harmony, and love. We can start with our family, friends, neighbours, and see how far one small act of kindness, one thoughtful word, one simple smile, can travel and what impact it can have.

From a distance, there is harmony
And it echoes through the land
And it's the hope of hopes It's the love of loves
It's the heart of every man

10th January 2025

Channel hopping on TV a few nights ago, I caught part of a programme that was discussing the differences between the generations, specifically the Baby Boomers and the Millennials. Now I didn't watch the rest of the programme, but it did get me thinking about how we define different generations, and in fact, how long is a generation? We all talk about past generations, but what do we actually mean? For much of history, we use the name of the reigning monarch to lump everyone together, the Victorians, lasting 60 years or so; the Georgians, lasting approximately 120 years; the Tudors, also approximately 120 years. But since 1945 (or 1900 in America), it has been generally accepted that 'a generation' covers all those born within a 15 – 20-year period.

So, I did a little bit of research and found lots and lots of websites that offer definitions for, and also suggested characteristics of, the generations born since the end of the Second World War.

Baby Boomers – 1946 – 1964 – Committed, self-sufficient, competitive, more likely to engage in face to face or phone conversations rather than text, non-tech savvy.

Generation X – 1965 – 1980 - Resourceful, logical, good problem solvers, straddling both the digital and non-digital worlds and confident in both.

Millennials (or Generation Y) – 1981 – 1995 – Confident, curious, questioning of authority, self-sufficient, tech savvy.

Generation Z – 1996 – 2010 – ambitious, digital-natives, confident, uncomfortable in verbal communication.

Generation Alpha – 2011 -? Until this generation reaches adulthood, no one can predict or guess their characteristics.

Reading through the definitions made me think about the horoscopes that appear in magazines and online, 'predicting' what millions of people who happen to be born around the same time of year will feel or experience that day, week, or month. It can't be done. Neither can everyone born over a 20-year period be defined by a title. I know Baby Boomers who are incredibly tech savvy, after all, the inventor of the World Wide Web was a Baby Boomer, and I also know members of Generation Z who love a good chin wag and will spend hours on the phone or face time talking to friends.

The only thing that defines each of us is our humanity, our individuality, and what we choose to do with the gifts and blessings we have. Fisherman's Friends, the Cornish Folk

Group, sing a wonderful song called 'Union of Different Kinds' which includes the line 'We're card-carrying lifelong members of the union of different kinds'

Our union is humanity, with all the variety, the individuality, the different races, genders, faiths, languages, that make up planet Earth. Whether you are a Baby-Boomer or a Millennial, Generation X or Generation Z, you are you, and you are special, valued, and loved. What you choose to do with all you have, and all you are, is up to you.

24th January 2025

Stand up for what you believe in, even if it means standing alone.

Have you ever been faced with the choice of continuing down the path you have chosen or turning back? Of taking the easy way out? Bishop Mariann Budde faced that choice on Tuesday when she mounted the steps into the pulpit in the National Cathedral in Washington, the day after the Inauguration of the President of the United States. If you have watched the service or seen clips of it on the news, you will have seen that moment played out as she paused, took a deep breath, and decided to carry on. To carry on down the path she had chosen, to carry on with her plea for mercy. Mercy for those people who are now scared. Scared for their lives, scared for their future, scared that their families will be broken up.

Now, whether you agree with all she said, some of it, or none of it, I hope we can agree that it took immense courage to make such a public appeal, and immense faith. She stood up for what she believed in, knowing that there would be consequences. One of the consequences she wakes up to every morning is the knowledge that there have been threats to her life, and the lives of her children and grandchildren.

But in an interview the day after, Bishop Budde said that she is not going to apologise because, as she said, 'I hope that a message calling for dignity, respecting dignity, honesty, humility and kindness is resonating with people'

Throughout history, there are numerous examples of people standing up for what they believe in, far too many to reflect on here. Some have been fighting for a cause, such as the suffragettes, some have been fighting for their country, such as the people of Ukraine, and some have been fighting for what they know to be right, such as the men and women who fought tirelessly to end the slave trade. Some have lost their lives in the fight, some have lost their freedom, and some have lost their homes. But what linked them all was that they were prepared to stand up for what they believe in, even if they stood alone.

I don't know if I would have had the courage to do what Bishop Budde did or to say what she said, in such a public arena, but it isn't a situation I will ever be faced with. But I hope and pray that I, that all of us, would have the courage to stand up for what we believe in, what we know to be right, and to accept the consequences. That we would stand up for the oppressed, the persecuted, the abused. That we would step in if we saw someone being attacked. That we would

340

challenge the bully, the racist, the oppressor. I pray that we would follow the example of the Good Samaritan and stop to help whoever, the person's faith, creed, or colour, and not pass by on the other side of the road. I pray that we would live up to the prayer of St Ignatius of Loyola.

Teach us, good Lord, to serve you as you deserve,
to give and not to count the cost,
to fight and not to heed the wounds, to toil and not to seek for rest,
to labour and not to ask for any reward, save that of knowing that we do your will.
Amen.

31st January 2025

Last week, at The Rectory, we decided to have a concerted and planned effort at decluttering (again). Having started with the books overloading my office shelves last year, and making a start on my clothes, we decided that we would tackle one kitchen cupboard a week, repurposing if possible, donating to Age UK charity shop if suitable (other charity shops are available), or simply throwing away (or, where we could, recycling of course.)

We began with the mug cupboard. First question, how many mugs do we really need? What is the maximum number of people we could comfortably offer hospitality to? Take that number, add 2 (in case of breakages), and get rid of the rest. The thing was, as soon as we had finished with the mugs, we were so in the zone that we decided to move on to the pots and pans. We have 4 spaces on the hob, allowing for a couple of pans to be in the wash; we only need a maximum of 6, so why did we have so many? (simple answer, we merged 2 households when we moved in, both of which had the maximum of practically everything). The baking cupboard was next. Cake, bread, and muffin tins were lined up, washed, and only some went back. It is amazing the amount of space we now have, and we are loving the fact that we can open a cupboard and don't risk a bump on the head from things falling out on us. The temporary downside is that the dining room is now full of boxes and bags waiting to make their way to their next home, but at least the kitchen looks and feels better. Next week it will be the dining room's turn, once the kitchen accumulation has been cleared, followed by the bathroom, and then the big one, the sitting room!

There are numerous articles, podcasts, even self-help books, that expound the virtues of decluttering, and many of us embrace the notion, especially in the New Year, as witnessed by the fact that this is not my first Ramble on the subject. But as with so many resolutions, we start off very enthusiastic but then 'life' gets in the way. There was no decluttering this week because we were both busy on our day off, heading off in different directions for the day, the evenings were full, and to be honest when we did have a few minutes of downtime it was feet up, cup of tea in hand, but we will get back to it next week, we are determined to get back to it next week.

The thing about resolutions, be it decluttering a room, or decluttering our lives and our minds, setting aside time to read, to pray, to meet up with friends more often, or to just have some 'me' time, is that the occasional 'falling off the wagon', so to speak, so often makes us stop, give up, throw in the towel, but it shouldn't. There are so many examples in the Bible of people starting off with the best of intentions, with resolution, with what seemed to be a faith beyond our wildest dreams, but who then gave up, gave in to fear, gave in to peer pressure. They could have so easily given up on their faith, on Jesus, even on life, but they didn't, and Jesus didn't give up on them.

So, whether as a New Years Resolution or a New You Resolution, you intended to declutter the home, decided to reduce your screen time, determined to go Eco, or resolved to deepen your faith and spiritual life, stick at it. If you miss a target, or a deadline, if you find that life is once again taking over, stop, take a deep breath, regroup, and start again. It will be worth it in the end.

7th February 2025

We've had a bit of a Tudor Fest recently. It started with a visit to CFT last week to see A Man for All Seasons, the Robert Bolt play telling the story of the final years in the life of Sir Thomas More, Henry VIII's chancellor, followed this week by the musical SIX (for the third time in as many years). Now even if you haven't seen it, or heard of it, it doesn't take much imagination to know it is about Henry's six wives.

The contrast between the two performances couldn't be greater, moving from the serious, and often wordy, play, to the high-octane, high-energy antics of the musical. But although they were two completely different experiences, they did also have some things in common, including the fact that they are both historically accurate. The musical tells the story of how each of the wives ended up with Henry, and how that association ended – Divorced, Beheaded, Died, Divorced, Beheaded, Survived. Each wife gets to tell her story in a 'competition' to decide which was the greatest, based on who suffered the most at Henry's hands. Now I hope it won't spoil it for you if you haven't seen it yet, if I tell you that the show ends with them coming together in unity to form a girl group called, predictably, SIX, and imaging how their lives would have been if they had said no to Henry's proposal. (OK, that bit isn't historically accurate but it is huge fun!)

The final song is a real high energy ear worm – it stayed with me all night and most of the next day! The audience are invited to stand, to dance, clapping along and even joining in. It is about the wives claiming back their own identity, as individuals, not just as one of the wives of Henry VIII - 'we're one of a kind, no category'.

It has got me thinking about how often we are identified by, put into, a category, and how often we do the same to others. How often because of our marital status, our job, even our skin colour, we are 'lumped together' and assumed to all think the same, behave the same, want the same things out of life. If someone supports Labour they think this way, Conservative that way. If you're single your life is like this, if you're married like that. If you're a doctor or a lawyer, a bus driver or a shop assistant, there is often an immediate, if subconscious, judgement made as to your intellect and your abilities! (If you have ever joined in the 1% Club on ITV you will know just how wrong those assumptions are!) The same assumptions are often made about people of faith as well.

Evangelicals think this, Anglo Catholics that. Baptists will behave this way, Roman Catholics that.

These assumptions, these prejudices, have no basis on what the individual is like, how they behave, what they believe, and it often comes as a shock when someone seems to break the mould, to do something we didn't expect, or think they were capable of.

Although I doubt the writers of SIX had St Paul in mind when they came up with the idea for the final song, it does reflect his words in his letter to the Galatians (3: 28) - 'There is neither Jew nor Gentile, neither slave nor free, nor is there male and female, for you are all one in Christ Jesus'. Of course, there are still Jews and Gentiles, and sadly there are still slaves, in fact more are now in Modern Slavery than at the height of the Slave Trade, but the title, the category, doesn't define them, or us. Yes, I know we have a new category, that of Christian, or as St Paul would have known it 'Followers of The Way', and that rightly comes with an expectation as to how we will behave, even if history has shown us how often we fail to live up to it, but we are still individuals within it, we are still one of a kind. We are us!

Isaiah (43: 1) tells us that God says 'I have called you by name, you are mine'. God doesn't lump us together under a category, under a social or economic group, he calls us and knows us as individuals, and it is as individuals, with our own hopes, dreams, doubts and fears, that we come to him as his children.

In SIX, the wives each reclaim their own identity whilst also acknowledging the lives and the strengths of each other. They come together to celebrate what makes them unique, what defines them as individuals, but also to recognise what unites them, just as we come together in worship before God, as individuals but united in faith. Oh, what a world it would be if we could all do the same, recognising each person's individuality whilst celebrating, and protecting, the humanity that unites us.

14th February 2025

When I worked as an office manager, I had to do an annual review and feedback to all my staff. It wasn't something I particularly enjoyed, and when I started I really struggled, but my manager told me to use the positive, negative, positive sandwich. I'm sure it is something many of you are familiar with, either in giving or receiving feedback. Start with the positive, then tackle what needs improvement or the negative, and then end with a positive. It is a great way of getting a message across without sending someone out feeling deflated. Of course it doesn't always work, and one of my staff always took away the positives but completely ignored the negatives!

I had my own positive, negative, positive experience this week. The week started with the Deanery Celebration of Faith. It was a wonderfully joyful evening, and Bishop Ruth spoke passionately about our faith, the Nicene Creed, and the Transfiguration. The people of Southbourne put on a wonderful spread for us afterwards, and we got to meet people from the other parishes in the Deanery, as well as chatting with both Bishop Ruth and Edward Dowler, the new Dean of the Cathedral.

My negative was partly my own fault, but after taking a call from a parishioner while at the shop on Wednesday, I had left my phone beside the till while I dealt with a customer. I had to leave the shop floor for a few minutes to search for his order, and when I couldn't find it, he made a quick exit promising to return later.

When I went to return my phone to the office, I found my debit cards had been stolen from the phone case. No damage was done, or money lost, because I immediately froze the cards and reported them stolen, but I spent the rest of the afternoon angry at him, and angry at myself for being so stupid. But then that evening I had the positive to complete the sandwich, a visit to CFT to watch 'Pride and Prejudice (sort of)', a clever and imaginative telling of the Jane Austen classic. I went to bed that night in a better frame of mind than I would have done if the negative experience was all I was focusing on.

We all have days, weeks, where we have positive and negative experiences, we all have times when we could let the negatives dominate, even let them take over our minds and lives so they colour everything else we do, but there are also always positives we can choose to embrace, or ignore. On Wednesday night I went to bed thanking God for the joy of the theatre experience, asking forgiveness for the very, very, negative thoughts that went through my mind about the opportunist thief, but also thankful for the technology that meant he only had the cards for a matter of minutes before they were cancelled and my money secure.

Now I admit, I don't always succeed in practising what I preach, my prayers at the end of the day are not always thankful, because sometimes I am also overwhelmed by a negative experience, by an off the cuff remark that hurts, by the death of a friend, but I know that God, through his Son, understands. I know that God loves me, loves us, and that it is because of our humanity, our faults and failings, as well as our joys and blessings, that he will always be there.

Our day-to-day experiences are what make us who we are, and it is our choice as to whether we see the negative everywhere, or the positive. It is our choice as to whether our future actions and judgements are based on bad experiences or good. My phone and handbag will now be locked away in the safe when I am at work, but my experience this week will not, I am determined, colour my judgement about people I meet. I will not see every customer as a potential thief, I will not question the motives of everyone I talk to. I am blessed in having more positive than negative times in my life, I am blessed in knowing more kind, generous, loving people, than mean, negative, people, and it is my experiences with them that keep me going, that keep me smiling, that keep me on the path that God wants me to follow – the be the best me I can be, and to give thanks.

21st February 2025

As I sit at my desk writing this Ramble, looking out at the grey sky, the trees and shrubs being buffered by the wind, it doesn't feel much like spring is on the way, but it is. The bulbs are pushing through, the snowdrops are still flowering, and there is new growth on the roses and the vine. The Met Office forecast that we would have higher temperatures than Greece this weekend, and although it doesn't feel like it today, I live in hope, although they did caveat the forecast with 'Greece is having an unusually cold snap at the moment'! But spring is on its way, with the promise of warmer weather, brighter skies, and longer days, as the mornings and evenings continue to get lighter.

Whilst the weather today is nothing like the storms we have seen over the past few months, it does seem quite pertinent that this Sunday, at both the main service and Children's Church, we are going to hear the story of Jesus stilling the storm, calming the waves and rebuking the wind. I love to imagine myself in the stories we hear of what Jesus did and said, and every time I hear this story, I can't help but smile to myself as I imagine Jesus telling the wind off, much like a parent might tell a child off for misbehaving, maybe with a bit of finger wagging, or a 'what did you do that for?'

question. Of course, we don't know exactly what Jesus did or said, if he actually said anything, to calm the storm, but whatever he did, it worked. Suddenly the disciples, and the crew, in the boat were no longer being tossed about, and they were no longer in fear – there was calm (Luke 8: 24).

It got me thinking about all the storms we have in our own lives, all the times we feel ourselves rocked by events, overwhelmed by situations, maybe even feel fear, if not for our lives as the disciples did, but maybe for our future, our jobs, our families. When we do feel fear, or uncertainty, or doubt, do Jesus' words to the disciples actually help? Once the waves had calmed, and the wind had dropped, Jesus turned to them and asked 'Where is your faith?'. For some people, that question suggests that if we have faith then we should never feel fear. If we have faith, we should never have doubts. If we have faith, we should never suffer the pains and grief that are part of being human.

But that isn't what it means. Jesus isn't saying that if the disciples had had faith they wouldn't have been hit by the storm, that if they had had faith, they wouldn't have felt fear. What Jesus is asking is where was their faith, their trust, in him and in God, to be there with them. To suffer with them, with us, to help calm the storms that are raging in our minds, even if the storm is still raging outside.

It is part of being human to have doubts and fears, as much as it is part of being human to have joys and hopes. Faith doesn't mean that life is always a bed of roses, it doesn't mean that the sun will always shine, but it does mean that whatever we are going through we are not alone. Jesus, the Son of God, didn't pop down to earth for a few years as a heavenly body, he lived amongst us for 33 years fully human. He laughed and cried as we do, he attended both weddings and funerals, as we do. And most importantly for me, he had doubts and questioned God, as we do.

On the night before he died, he asked God to take away the cup of death, but then accepted 'thy will be done' On the cross, he cried out 'My God, My God, why have you forsaken me', but then, with faith and the knowledge that he had not been abandoned, he bowed his head and said 'It is finished'.

We, like creation, have cold, dark days, but we also have warm, bright days, we have times of doubt and times of certainty, but through it all we have a constant companion who knows first had what life is like. One who knows and understands that sometimes our faith is strong, and sometimes he needs to prod us and ask, 'Where is your faith?' But all the time loving us and walking with us in whatever life throws at us, ready to bring calm, ready to give us peace.

28th February 2025

I was never in the Guides, or the Brownies for that matter, but I, along with most people, I'm sure, am well aware of the motto of both the Guides and the Scouts, Be Prepared! The badges that they earn prepare them for all sorts of situations in life, First Aid, Fire Safety, Conservation, Crafts, to name but a few of the hundreds that are available, and teach them the skills they may need, but also increase their knowledge and awareness of the world around them. They also learn skills for which I'm not sure there is a badge, although I am happy to be corrected, the skill of working with others, and the skill of engaging with people of all ages and all backgrounds. They learn the value and importance of being kind, of sharing, of helping others. They are being prepared.

On Wednesday, Christians around the world, of all denominations and traditions, begin the Season of Lent. It is a season where the focus is often on repentance and on sacrifice, but it is also a season of preparation. We are preparing ourselves for the events of Holy Week, and especially the events of the Triduum, Maundy Thursday, Good Friday, and Holy Saturday. The forty days of Lent (which don't include Sundays) reflect the 40 days that Jesus spent in the wilderness before he began his ministry in earnest. For 30 years, Jesus knew that he was the Son of God, born fully human, as well as fully divine, to save us from ourselves, but those 30 years were not his time of preparation. Yes, he astounded the priests in the Temple of Jerusalem at a young age with his knowledge and understanding (Luke 2: 41 – 52), yes, some believe he had already begun to look for his disciples, but that was all during a time of waiting.

Waiting for the right time, waiting for the sign from God that he was ready. That sign was John the Baptist, sent to 'prepare the way of the Lord'. John's Baptism ministry, and specifically his Baptism of Jesus, was the green light for Jesus to put his head above the parapet, or to use an athletics analogy, Jesus had been in the blocks, and John's baptism was the firing of the starting pistol.

But what did Jesus do the minute he was baptised, what was the first act of his newly confirmed position, 'This is my Son, the Beloved, in whom I am well pleased' (Matthew 3: 17). He was led, or driven according for some translations of the Bible, out in to the wilderness for forty days and forty nights. This was his preparation time. This was the time, and space, he needed to focus, to really understand, discern, what he had to do. He was tempted by the Devil (Matthew 4: 1 – 11) to turn stones into bread, to jump from the pinnacles of the Temple to test if God would save him, and he was offered a way out of all that was to follow if he would only swear allegiance to the Devil. Jesus's forty days in the wilderness not only strengthened his resolve, but also strengthened his faith. They prepared him for what was to come.

This Lent I don't know yet what I am going to sacrifice, time, money, chocolate, cheese, and I don't know what I am going to take on, more bible reading, more prayer time, but I pray that whatever I do, whatever you do, will be done not for my own self-satisfaction, look at me aren't I good, but for the glory of God and as a true time of preparation for the dark day of Good Friday, the day of waiting on Holy Saturday, and then the celebration of the glorious resurrection on Easter Day.

But I also pray that this Lent we don't just prepare ourselves for Easter, but like the Guides and Scouts, we also prepare ourselves for all that life may throw at us in the future, that we prepare ourselves, arm ourselves, with the gifts and skills that God has given us to be kind, to be welcoming, to be the best us we can be, all with the knowledge that Jesus knows what it is like to be human, and is walking with us every day.

14th March 2025

One of my favourite films at Christmas, well at any time really, is 'It's a Wonderful Life', with James Stewart. I'm sure most of you know the film, but a quick resume of the story line is that as George contemplates ending his life and wishing he had never been born, a Guardian Angel called Clarence is sent from God to show him all the good he has done, all the lives he has changed, all the people he has helped. Through various events, re-imaging what would have happened if George hadn't been born, Clarence shows him just how much he means to the people of Bedford Falls, and beyond. Just how much of an impact he has had, even without knowing it.

You may be wondering why I am referencing a Christmas film as we make our way through Lent. Well, we have sadly had a number of deaths in the Valley Parish recently, and every time I have the privilege of being asked to lead the service, or I attend a funeral as a mourner, I am reminded of the first funeral I ever led, and of 'It's a Wonderful Life', and I find myself wishing we all had a Guardian Angel like Clarence.

The first funeral I ever led was in 2016, and it was sadly for a young woman, whom I will call Mary, who had taken her own life. The family was in shock, and was unable to answer the question they, and her friends, really needed answering – Why? There was no simple answer, and there was nothing more anyone could have done to help her, but as we all sat in church and listened to her friends and work colleagues tell of all she had done, in her life, and to help others, to say how much she had meant to them, her Mum leant over to me and said 'I wish Mary could have heard all this'. Speaking to the family afterwards, they acknowledged that their daughter's mental health issues were severe, and perhaps nothing could have changed the outcome, but it would have been good if she could have known, just like George, what a positive impact she had had on so many other people's lives.

Every time I hear friends and family speak at a funeral, or exchange anecdotes at a wake, I am reminded of Mary, and of 'It's a wonderful life', and I want to ask those people, but I never do, did you tell them? Did you tell your Mum, your brother, your friend, how much they meant to you? Did you tell your work colleague how important they had been to you, how much you had learnt from them? Even if you didn't say it, did they know how much you loved them?

I'm sorry if this is a little maudlin, and I'm not trying to make anyone feel guilty. In my experience, we are all very capable of rethinking, overthinking, our relationships, and worrying about whether the person we have just lost did know how much we loved them, without someone else putting their oar in and making us doubt even more. If you're worried if they knew, the chances are, they did, because you wouldn't worry if you hadn't cared, and you can't care and not show it in some way.

I'm also not suggesting that we all go overboard in telling everyone we know, all the time, how much they mean to us, but I hope this is a gentle nudge to say it, occasionally. To show it, occasionally. An unexpected bunch of flowers, or pint down the pub. A cup of coffee for the work colleague who has just got you out of a jam. A phone call to that friend you haven't spoken to in ages, but who has been there for you through thick and thin. A simple thank you to the postie, the delivery driver. A simple thank you, a simple compliment, time spent listening, really listening, to them, is all it takes most of the time for someone to know they are appreciated, to know they are loved. And who knows, if they do the same, if we all do the same, we could change the world.

362

21st March 2025

I've recently been watching a Lucy Worsley series on the rise and fall of the Boleyn family, based almost entirely on letters they wrote, received, or that were written about them. The letter Edward VIII wrote to abdicate changed British history, and the famous letter of Elizabeth I, written to her sister as she was taken to the Tower of London, shows us not only her state of mind, but the intrigue that surrounded her as she drew diagonal lines under her words to prevent anyone adding 'incriminating comments'. Letters written from the front line in both World Wars, as well as the Boer War and more recently during the Troubles in Northern Ireland and the Second Gulf War, give us a unique insight into the thoughts, and fears, of the ordinary soldiers.

I've been prompted to think about the 'lost art' of letter writing, and of Pen Pals, by the talk at the WI last night. West Dean school is looking at ways to create closer links with the school in Xilitla, Mexico. The village was home to Edward James for many years whilst he built the famous Las Pozas gardens, and the schools are keen to build on their shared history. Plans for regular Zoom calls and internet exchanges are having to be rethought as the Mexican school doesn't have the technology, and so, as the Head Teacher at West

Dean said, 'it may have to be by letter'. The joy and gift of Pen Pals.

When I was at school, many years ago, I had a couple of Pen Pals, one in France and one in Italy. Sadly, our communications didn't last long as we, along with so many of our friends, got overwhelmed by exams and study, and the joys of socialising, but I know that for a small number the letter exchange continued for many years, and may even be still ongoing, and I am slightly envious of them.

There is, I have to say, something wonderful about receiving, and writing, a hand written letter. Unlike an email or text, the person writing has had to take time. They have had to concentrate not only on what they are saying but, especially in my case, on making sure the writing is legible (my Dad always said I had the handwriting of a doctor! No offence to doctors). Once posted, it is then a case of waiting for a reply. How long before we start to wonder if it has been received, two days, three? How long before we start to wonder if anything is wrong – one week, two? And then the joy of the reply, of having something tangible in our hands to read and reread, to maybe keep forever.

As famous as Elizabeth I's letter is, and as likely as it is to be preserved for hundreds of years, there are other letters that are older, and have had a greater impact on the world. The letters of St Paul, St Peter, and others, found in the New Testament. These letters, Epistles, are both inspiring and frustrating. Inspiring because they teach us more about faith, and about living that faith, but also frustrating because we can only guess at what prompted their writing. What was in the letters the Apostles received? What was going on in the churches and house groups around the known world that needed the intervention, the encouragement, sometimes the reproach, of the leaders of the early Church? I can't help but wonder how the people of Corinth, Rome, Philippi felt as they waited for that letter – waited weeks, even months, to hear back from St Paul. The excitement, anticipation, maybe even trepidation, they felt as they gathered together to hear it read to them. How those who could read poured over the letter, shared it with family and friends. How they protected them, reread them, and used them for teaching and preaching as we still do today.

I hope and pray that the children of West Dean and the children of Xilitla embrace the idea of letter writing. I hope they come to know the joy of Pen Pals, and I hope they also come to learn a little of the thrill, the anticipation, of waiting. Waiting for that letter to drop through the letter box, or to be given out in class. And I hope, like the Epistles, that they are shared, that they learn from them about life in other parts of the world as we have learnt about the people of Corinth, Rome, and that they are kept, so that future generations, maybe their own children, will also be able to understand a little more about life in The Valley, and in Mexico, in 2025, and beyond.

28th March 2025

In the book 'Tales from an Undergardener' by Richard Littledale, the writer offers a reflection, every day, on a bible passage in relation to the writer's garden, what is growing, what is not, what worked in other gardens that doesn't in his current location. In today's offering, the writer reflects on how we judge people, consciously or unconsciously, by what they are wearing, how they speak, and what they look like. His analogy was the birds in his garden. He loved seeing the robins, wrens, and sparrows at his feeder. The occasional visit from a woodpecker prompted him to get out his binoculars or camera, and like us, he loved seeing the odd pheasant hoovering up the fallen seeds under the feeder. But then it came to the rooks, crows, and pigeons. He didn't want them in his garden. Like is. He would wave his arms to shoo them away, or open the window to scare them off. Why? They are birds, just like the wrens, and they need to feed, just like the pheasants, but they just didn't fit in. He found the dawn chorus lifted his spirits, until again the rooks joined in and their calls grated on the ear, but why? They were all saying the same thing, just with a different accent.

If you watched the latest series of Traitors, you will know that one of the traitors, Charlotte, faked a Welsh accent for the whole series because it is 'more trustworthy'. In the second of the Downton Abbey films, a silent movie star bemoans the fact that 'talkies' would mean the end of her career because she had a strong London accent, unacceptable to the film makers of Hollywood who wanted a crisp, clean-cut upper-class accent. In a restaurant, a group wearing shirts and ties, with the women in dresses, will often get a 'better table' than the group of young mums in jeans and tee shirts, and then there is the classic scene from Pretty Woman. A posh upmarket boutique on Rodeo Drive refuses to serve Julia Robert's character because she isn't dressed right, she isn't 'the right sort'. Oh, what wonderful revenge when after spending a small fortune at another shop, the character re-enters the store, overloaded with bags, reminds the sales assistant that she wouldn't serve her, and then says, 'Big mistake. Big. Huge!'

And we don't have to look that far back in our history to remember times when we have seen or heard, or been guilty ourselves, a judgement based on how someone sounds or looks. At the height of The Troubles in Northern Ireland, an Irish accent was viewed with suspicion; were they a member of the IRA? In early 2020, you only had to walk down East Street in Chichester to see people move away from anyone who looked even vaguely Chinese, did they have Covid?

And in recent weeks, I know Americans who claim to be Canadian if asked, because they don't want to be judged on the actions of their leaders.

In the letter from the apostle James in the Bible (James 2: 2 – 4), he tackles this discrimination, this judgement of others by their dress, by how they look, head on.

'My brothers and sisters, believers in our glorious Lord Jesus Christ must not show favouritism. Suppose a man comes into your meeting wearing a gold ring and fine clothes, and a poor man in filthy old clothes also comes in. If you show special attention to the man wearing fine clothes and say, "Here's a good seat for you," but say to the poor man, "You stand there" or "Sit on the floor by my feet," have you not discriminated among yourselves and become judges with evil thoughts?'

We are all guilty, to a greater or lesser degree, of unconscious bias. Of making decisions and judgements about someone based on their accent, their clothes, their skin colour, without getting to know them, without understanding them, and it takes a very conscious decision, a very conscious mind change, to stop ourselves, but it is worth the effort, because one day it may be God asking us why we didn't serve that person, why we didn't include that person,

why we didn't help that person, and it will be Him saying
'Big mistake. Big. Huge!'

11th April 2025

Holy Week

On Sunday, we, along with all Christians around the world, will be celebrating Palm Sunday, the day Jesus rode triumphantly into Jerusalem on a donkey. As I have rambled on before, it is believed that as Jesus entered Jerusalem by one gate, Pilate was entering by another, on the other side of the city. Their entries could not have been more different. Jesus, humbly, on a donkey, surrounded by his disciples and met by cheering crowds, Pilate, arrogantly, probably on a charger, surrounded by Roman soldiers and met by the leaders of the Temple.

The story of the two different arrivals always reminds me of a story I was told a few years ago by a colleague in a different diocese. It may be true, it may be an urban myth, but it does make a good story. A small-town church was holding a service to rededicate the building after being closed for several months while a new floor was laid. They had invited the Bishop to officiate and had also invited all of the local dignitaries, including the Mayor of the nearby city. The

371

Churchwardens had put someone on look out at the entrance to the car park to make sure they were there to greet the Bishop when he arrived. As the lookout saw a large, imposing car turn into the car park, he ran back to the church and announced, 'The Bishop is here!'. The Parish Priest and Churchwardens rushed out to greet him and waited at the Lynch Gate. As they headed out, they barely noticed the seemingly insignificant cyclist locking up his bike and heading into the church. As the car door opened, a voice could be heard calling to them as the lookout ran from the church 'The Bishop is here'! The Churchwardens waved him away as they smiled to greet, The Mayor! The Bishop, much like Bishop Martin, used public transport and his bike as much as he could, and had arrived under the radar, humbly riding a bike.

Now I'm not saying the Mayor was arrogant, he was probably as surprised by the greeting as the welcome party was by who alighted from the car, but it does make me think about how often we look at the externals to decide who is important and who isn't. I know it has been 5 years since we were first under Covid restrictions, but what that time taught us was that it wasn't the CEO's who were important, it wasn't the bankers or the celebrities who kept the country going, it was the refuse collectors, the shop assistants, the nurses. The people who probably arrived at work by foot, by bike, or by public transport, unassumingly going about their day-to-day duties.

As we enter Holy Week, as we celebrate Jesus' humble arrival in Jerusalem on Palm Sunday, his act of service on Maundy Thursday in washing the disciples' feet, and his ultimate sacrifice for us on Good Friday, I pray that we will all remember that he came to serve, and not to be served, and commit ourselves to do the same, humbly, unassumingly, simply, loving one another as he loves us.

Printed in Dunstable, United Kingdom

70248021R00211